AF398575

# Gino Leineweber (Ed.)

# Spring's Blue Ribbon

## International Poetry

Verlag Expeditionen

Publisher: Verlag Expeditionen, 2021
Spring's Blue Ribbon
International Poetry
Edited by Gino Leineweber

Printed in Germany

Cover Design: Birgitta Sjöblom
Foto: erikreis
ISBN 978-3-947911-57-8

*Spring lets flutter its blue ribbon*
*Through the air again*

Eduard Mörike, German poet (1804-1875)

# Poetry from

# Spring's Blue Ribbon

# International Poetry

# Prologue

I am pleased to present the fourth international poetry anthology, and I thank all my worldwide poet friends for their contributions to this book. This poetry collection contains poems from 60 poets and 20 countries on five out of seven continents.

Poetry is one, if not the oldest, form of literary expression. And for many centuries, it was the most important form of literature.

Today, it is a kind of niche art. But it is still as crucial to understanding the world as it was in the early days. Poetry is written for the public, for an audience. And poetry does what it has always done. It uses images and metaphors to convey a picture of our world and to understand what's going on around and inside us. Poetry is the purest form of literature. In it, you see a world without boundaries.

That is what poetry means: to look at everything with the eyes of an open mind. That's why it is an honor for me to present poems to you from different areas, countries, and cultures.

These poems are published in their native language and in American English. Through these translations in one particular language, it is possible to imagine their unique spirit in the original tongue.

The collection's theme is spring: the season or the idea of spring in a metaphorical sense, i.e., seeing people or things changed or in transition, making them better.

The book's title refers to an excellent spring poem by the German poet Eduard Mörike (1804-1875) with its famous lines "Spring lets its blue ribbon/Flutter in the breeze again."
I hope that in curating this book, we have created a collection of poems that contains a gem for every lover of poetry.
I wish you much pleasure reading this book!

Gino Leineweber
October 2021

14

# POEMS

# SO SO, FRÜHLING
*Albrecht Classen, USA/Deutschland*


Lange hatte es gedauert,
der Winter war so hart,
kalt und windig
blies er um das Haus,
viel mehr Schnee als gewünscht,
warum wollte er nicht enden?
Trotzdem gab es Winterspaß,
die Natur unter weißer Decke.

Lang ist's her,
ein so bittrer Winter,
heute ist es viel zu warm
auf der erhitzten Erde,
Frühling kommt
und eilt vorbei,
globale Transformation.

Blaue Bänder
flattern dahin,
die gelben Blütenschauer
trudeln schnell
ihres Weges,
und schon ist es viel zu heiß,
wo sind denn die Bänder geblieben?

Frühlingsschauer
bleiben aus,
trocken starrt der Garten
erstickt vor sich hin,
Veilchen wachsen nicht,

von Narzissen ist gar nicht die Rede.
das bisschen Grün,
wo mag es geblieben sein,
und Mörikes poetischen Ton
vermag ich nicht zu hören.

Wenn da etwas flattert,
sind es Plastiktüten im Wind,
ein wenig Regen wäre ja ganz schön,
darauf wirst du lange warten,
sprich mir bloß von Frühling nicht
der Sommer hat uns längst im Griff
und dies nicht allein
in unsrer Sonora Wüste.

## SPRING, REALLY?
*Albrecht Classen, USA/Germany*

It had lasted for long,
the winter had been so hard,
cold and windy
it blew around the house,
more snow than desired,
why did it not finally end?
But there had also been winter joys,
nature asleep under the blanket white.

It has been a long time ago,
such a bitter winter,
today it is much too warm
on the heated mother earth,
Spring arrives
and rushes by,
global transformation.

Blue bands
fly past us rushingly,
the yellow petal showers
trundle so fast
leaving us behind,
and then the heat sets in,
where have all the bands disappeared?

The Spring showers
are staying away,
the garden stares at us
without any breathing,
violets do not grow here,

and forget the daffodils,
the little green
where might it have gone,
and Mörike's poetic sound
is not audible to me.

If anything might flatter
then the plastic bags in the wind,
a little rain would really be nice,
yet you will have to wait for it long,
just do not talk to me about Spring,
we are already in the Summer's stronghold
and this not only
in our Sonoran Desert.

" مغادرة "
علي الحازمي - السعودية

بالمطارات ورد الكلام يجفُّ سريعاً
حمام عيونٍ يحط على شرفات وجوه
، يخاطب سِفْرَ عذوبتها في التياع مرير
أنامل ثلج تذوب بدفء كفوفٍ
، تشدُّ عليها أمانٍ أخيرة
بعض حقائب حزنٍ من الجلد تبدو مهيأةً
، للتقيؤ بعد سماع النداء الأخير

أيادٍ تلوّح للدمع أن يتساقط
، من شجر باذخٍ في الضلوع
قلوب تغادر أجساد أحبابها
في مقاعد مائلةٍ للرحيل
رحيقٌ من القبلات يسافر في وجنةٍ
، قد أتمت رباط حزام الأمان إلى خصرها
نهر فوضى يمدُّ غصون هتافات سابحةٍ
في بياض ضمائرها أو يبدد آخر وقتٍ
لمعنى العناق السريع على ضفةٍ تنثني
ولأن المسافات آخذة في تلاشي عيون
تتوق انعتاقاً إلى مثلها
كم تظل ورود الكلام مجففةً
فوق أرض المدرَّج
في خيبة

## DEPARTURE
*Ali Al Hazmi, Saudi Arabia*


At airports,
Roses of words dry up so rapidly;
Birds of the eyes, falling upon the terraces of the
faces,
Address the verses of their purity in bitter longing;
Icy fingers melt in the warm hands,
Grasping the last wishes,
For the last time.
Leather bags of sadness seem ready for vomiting
Upon hearing the last call.
Hands urge the tears to fall down from the sublime
trees
Blooming in the ribs.

Hearts depart the bodies of dear persons
On seats about to fly.
A nectar of kisses traveling on a cheek
That has already fastened the safety belt to its waist.
A river of chaos mingles with cries
Swimming in the whiteness of their conscience,
And wastes the last minutes of quick last hugs
On a receding shore.
Since distances are diminishing in the eyes dreaming
of a similar flight,
The roses of words will stay on the airport floor,
Lifeless and dried up,
In complete despair.

# MASKENBALL
*Anna Würth, Deutschland*


Die kahlen Äste
sehnender Bäume
noch malen sie
ihr Craquelé
ins blaueste Blau
kein Flieger nirgends
auf der Himmelsbühne
im Lockdown-Frühling
zwanzigzwanzig
Da oben Tanz in Schwarz
hier unten Maskenball in Moll
immerhin mit blauem Band im Haar

Zu früh zu laut im Morgengrau
doch hoffnungshell
vertrau dem Vogelruf
der deine Nacht vertreibt
mit gefiedertem Radau

Wirf ihn ab
den Winterkokon
Raum für freches Grün

# THE MASKED DANCER
*Anna Würth, Germany*
*Translated by John Waterfield,*
*United Kingdom*

The bare branches
of yearning trees
still paint their craquelure
into the bluest of blues
no planes on the sky stage
anywhere
in lockdown spring
twenty twenty
Up there a dance in black
down here masked ball in minor
at least with a blue ribbon in my hair

Too early too loud
in the grey dawn
but bright with hope
trust the bird call
that drives away your night
with feathered rumpus

Cast it off
the winter cocoon
make room for frisky green

# EL PAÍS DE LA INFANCIA
### *Annabel Villar, Uruguay/España*

Nuevamente es octubre
tiempo de tilos y lluvia con sol.

Van rodando por las calles
–alfombradas por las flores del plátano–
las imágenes del viento
y las pequeñas partículas
de una primavera que ha regresado
perpetua y escandalosamente loca.

Y yo agradezco el sabor de los rojos
y los contornos nítidos del mundo
y que mis ojos se asfixien
con el intenso milagro
de las tormentas de luz.

# HOMELAND OF CHILDHOOD
*Annabel Villar, Uruguay/Spain*

Once again it is October
time of linden and rain with sunshine.

Rolling down the streets
–which are carpeted in plan-tree flowers–
images of the wind
and the small particles
of a spring that has returned
perpetually and scandalously insane.

And I am grateful for the taste of reds
and the sharp outlines of the world,
and that my eyes suffocate
with the intense miracle
of storms of light.

# UNVERNÄHTE FÄDEN
*Antje Stehn, Deutschland*


Schau mal die Samen
des Jasmins in ihrer Schote
auf engstem Raum einer neben den
anderen gefaltet
ununterscheidbar stummes Leben
nimm sie aus der Schale!
Wort für Wort
einzelne Stimmen in Form eines Fallschirms
suchen ihren Landeplatz

Freiheit!
ein schönes Wort
ein Pulloverwort
hunderte male mit sicherer Hand
über den Kopf gezogen
plötzlich falsch herum
unvernähte Fäden baumeln
um die Utopie
einer offenen Gesellschaft

# UNSTITCHED THREADS
*Antje Stehn, Germany*


I'd like to show you the seeds
of jasmine in their husk
lying in the minimum space
folded one on top of the other
indistinguishable silent life
peel them from their pod!
word by word
isolated voices in the  form of a parachute
seeking their landing site

Freedom!
a nice word, isn't it?
a sweater word
pulled over the head
hundreds of times with a sure hand
suddenly it's the wrong way around
unstitched threads dangle
round the utopia
of an open society

# ΕΑΡΙΝΗ ΠΡΟΒΟΛΗ
*Αριστέα Παπαλεξάνδρου, Ελλάδα*

I
Ήταν σκοτεινιασμένος
ο ουρανός του ονείρου
Μετά ξημέρωσε
σκοτεινιασμένη μέρα

Άνδρες γυναίκες συρροή
αγνώστων συντροφίες
Αυτός ο κύριος αυτή
με τον λευκό λαιμό
Αυτός ο κύριος αυτή
— Με το μαύρο περίστροφο
Φιγούρες δίχως βλέμμα
μου γνέφουν μου μιλούν
Τους σέρνω όλους στη δουλειά
στη μυστική συνάντηση
με τον εντεταλμένο
του μεσιτικού στη γενική
συνέλευση στην εφορία
Πουλώ το βιος μου ξεπουλώ
σάλες γεμάτες τράπεζες
λαμπρές οινοποσίες

του ύπνου μου του ξύπνου μου
εμένα σώμα και ψυχή
υπάρχοντά μου όλα
με πουλώ με ξεπουλώ
υπάρχοντά μου
παρελθόν

αυτός με τον λευκό λαιμό
με το μαύρο περίστροφο
Φιγούρες

αεικίνητες
καλά κρυμμένα
μυστικά
γλίτωσαν όλοι
Κι ο δολοφόνος του φονιά
στο πιο ωραίο άλλοθι
μακριά στην Γουαδελούπη
Γλίτωσαν όλοι
πλην εμού
που τους ονειρευόμουν




II
Έως εδώ το όνειρο
και τώρα η προφητεία

Ύπνοι χωρίς ενύπνια
Φθινόπωρο χωρίς βροχή
Τσιγάρο στον ακάλυπτο
Γυμνή το καταχείμωνο
Κανείς να μη ζεσταίνεται
Κανείς να μην κρυώνει
Από παντού να βρέχεσαι
Από παντού να καίγεσαι
Άθικτος όπως πριν
Να παραμένεις

Ώστε
δεν είμαι μόνη,
καλά το είπες
Και προπαντός
που δεν περίμενες
ο κόσμος σου να φωτιστεί
από έναν κάποιο ήλιο

# SPRINGTIME PROJECTION
*Aristea Papalexandrou, Greece*
*Translated by Philip Ramp, USA/Greece*

I
Dream's sky
was overcast
Then an overcast day
broke as well

Men women a throng
companionship of strangers
This gentleman this
white throated woman
This man, her
—With the black revolver
Figures sightless
nodding at speaking to me
I'm dragging all of them off to work
to a secret meeting
with the one authorized
by the brokerage to the general
assembly to the tax office
I'm selling my life selling it off
salons tables packed in tight
resplendent libations

of my sleep my waking
me myself body and soul
all my belongings
I'm selling, selling myself off
my belongings
past
the man with the white throat
with the black revolver
Figures

perpetually moving
well hidden
secrets
everyone was saved
And the assassin of the murderer
the most beautiful alibi
far away in Guadeloupe
Everyone was saved
except me
who was dreaming of them


II
The dream up to here
from here on prophecy

Sleep without dream
Autumn without rain
Cigarette out in the open
Her naked, dead of winter
No one not getting warm
No one not getting cold
You're rained on from all sides
You're seared on all sides
Remaining untouched as
You were before


Therefore
I am not alone,
you were right
And in any case
when you least expect it
your world is illuminated
by some kind of sun

PAN

*Ayça Erdura, Türkiye*

Beyaz çökmüş kıra
Kıran girmiş sanki çiçeğe
İhtişamı yakın flütün
Yakın doygun arzuların uykusu

Gökdelenleri hızlı trenleri metroları merdivenleri çatıları
Sallayarak gelen kim
Döken sıvaları tuğlaları kıran parkeleri söken camları
döven

Deniz nerde
Kayın ağaçlarını demiyle besleyen
Kayın ki yaprakları büyüktür yeşili başka
Gölgesi yakındır çocuğa

Okulları servisleri dersleri birikmiş betonları
dolapları çantaları
Fırlatıp atan kim
Kırkbirnoktabir knot güney batı yönünden suyu yoran
havayı süren

Kıvrık çift boynuzlu
Tutam sakalıyla otururken köprü başında
Pan flütü çalan söyle
Keçimi kim bulacak benim

PAN
  *Ayça Erdura, Turkey*
  *Translated by Tozan Alkan, Turkey*

A whiteness covered the fields
And destroyed all the flowers
The glory of the flute was near
So was the sleep of contented desires

Who's coming
Shaking skyscrapers high-speed trains subways
stairs roofs
Scratching wall plasters breaking bricks removing
parquet floors hitting glasses

Where is the sea
Feeding beech trees with its breath
Those beeches whose leaves are big
and particularly green
And shadows are closer to a child

Who's throwing out
Schools buses lessons masses of concrete closets
bags
Forty-one-point-one knots from southwest tiring
water leading air

You, curved double-horned
Sitting on the bridge with a pinch of beard
And playing the flute
Tell me who will find my goat

## APRIL
*Betty Gilmore, USA*


April was not the cruelest
month
even in spite of the rain
for the grey slowly turned
to blue
and we learned to look up again
to see the white clouds that
floated about
like good memories
we'd left behind
and even if they lasted so briefly
a week, a month, a day
inside them we found a pleasure
that never stayed away.
And bright flowers soothed
us in summer.

# SPRING
*Betty Gilmore, USA*


There are places
on our tiny little earth
that some people
have never seen
like deserts or icebergs
or tropical islands
or even a season called
spring.

Some of us had the good fortune
to see it arrive every year
together with winter summer
and fall
but now we've made
such a mess of it all
that now we don't exactly
know
when spring will come
and if it does where will it go?
And will we still call it Spring?

# STREUBLUMEN
*Burkhard P. Bierschenck, Deutschland*

Wegen Dir
sitz ich hier
und esse Tulpen,
rot und gelb.

Im Busch
pfeift ein Pirol
eine Melodie
ohne Moll.

Frisch gemähte
Wiese mit bunten
Streublumen.
Ich niese.

# SPREAD FLOWERS
*Burkhard P. Bierschenck, Germany*


Because of you
I sit here
and eat tulips,
Red and yellow

In the bush
an oriole whistles
a melody
without a minor key.

Freshly mown
meadow with colorful
scattered flowers.
I sneeze

## ΟΤΑΝ Η ΑΝΟΙΞΗ ΑΡΓΕΙ
*Χλόη Κουτσουμπέλη, Ελλάδα*

Όταν η Άνοιξη αργεί
τα χωράφια αναπνέουν με δυσκολία
κάτω από το λευκό σεντόνι του νεκροτομείου
τα φρούτα βαλσαμωμένα
τα πουλιά ταριχευμένα
οι αρκούδες λιπόθυμες
και κάτω από το δέρμα του δάσους
κοιμάται το φίδι των εποχών
σκέφτομαι την Κάτω  Γη
εκεί που τα βλέφαρα σου
μικρές συμπληγάδες τρυφερότητας
έχουν κλείσει αμετάκλητα
εκεί που τα ψάρια μετεωρίζονται
μικρά αερόστατα με γυάλινα μάτια
εκεί που η Άνοιξη μένει πάντα σφραγισμένη
στο μπουκάλι της σαμπάνιας
που ο φελλός του δεν θα εκτοξευτεί ποτέ.

Γιατί Άνοιξη είναι το σώμα του αγαπημένου
και η μνήμη του ανθίζει αιώνια.

# WHEN SPRING DELAYS
*Chloe Koutsoubelli, Greece*


When Spring delays
and the fields breath with difficulty
under the white sheet of the morgue
the fruits are embalmed
the birds mummified
the bears have passed out
and under the skin of the forest
sleeps the snake of time,
I am thinking of the Underneath Land
where your eyelids
small Symplegades of tenderness
have clashed irrevocably
where fish levitate
small aerostats with huge eyes made of glass
where Spring is forever sealed
in a champagne bottle
whose cork will never explode.

Because Spring is the lover's body
and its memory eternally blooms .

neu geboren
*Christine Geweke, Deutschland*


ein junger tag zuhause in der welt
neugeboren und unschuldig
zart natur atmet (wie jeder frühling)
himmlischer hauch im irdisch haus

die welt mir anvertraut, all die ängste
sie nähren meine kunst zu leben. in
jungfräulichen stunden pflanze ich vers
an vers aus wachstum, wärme und licht

tagsüber aufbruchstimmung - nachts
blühende tage im traume - und trost

new born
*Christine Geweke, Germany*
*Translated by Benjamin Geweke, Germany*

a young day at home in the world
newborn and innocent
tender nature breathes (like every spring)
heavenly breath in the earthly house

the world entrusted to me, all the fears
they nourish my art to live. in
virgin hours i plant verse
to verse from growth, warmth and light

during the day a mood of departure – at night
blooming days in dreams – and solace

# GOSOKA KORWA RIBURU RIE'GETAGE
*Christopher Okemwa, Kenya*

torosa, gose oite egekoe
korusia moyo
nakoiranana
engaki yobuoba
yaerire, imagega ere
engaki enyia yaachire
okwegena okoyia
guachakire gokina
ime yaito
omorero bwokire
omogaso
ore ase ebitunwa biaito
chinyoni ngotera chire
obonyasi bwamerire ebitii
ense yabeire buya
oguanchana
okomunyuntana
okogoka
ogochaka okoyia
engaki enyia

# COMING OUT OF SECLUSION
*Christopher Okemwa, Kenya*

Don't tire, or breathe in
the air of desperation
or dark pessimism
a season of fear
is now behind us
spring is yonder
new fresh buds of hope
are beginning to grow
in the core of our being
a new fire has sprung
the sunlight
is bright upon the hills
the birds are able to sing again
fields are spread with fresh grass
the earth is back to life
the hugging
the kissing
the partying
a new beginning
a season of spring

# GERANI ALLA FINESTRA
*Claudia Piccinno, Italia*

Incombe
lo sfarfallio di morte
mentre scorre la vita alla finestra...
Sul davanzale ancora un geranio.
Resiste alle intemperie
il bucaneve su in montagna.
E si domanda l'aquila
perché il cielo è cosi azzurro
pur piovendo lacrime da giorni
su chi scruta le nubi col naso all'insù.
Creatura della fede
o delirio collettivo
una madre pietosa
ha fatto capolino
per trascinare in salvo i suoi bambini.
Sia essa scienza, humanitas
O chissà...
Noi gerani alla finestra
proviamo a trarre linfa
da questo lungo inverno.
La primavera è giunta
smarrendo i suoi colori.

# GERANIUM AT THE WINDOW
*Claudia Piccinno, Italy*

Incumbent was
the flicker of death
while life flew through the window...
On the windowsill one more geranium.
Withstands bad weather the snowdrop
high in the mountains.
And the eagle wonders
why the sky is so blue
despite it was raining tears for days
on who scrutinizes the clouds
with upturned nose.
Creature of faith or collective delusion
a pitiful mother peeped to drag safely her children.
Be it science, humanitas
Or who knows...
We geraniums at the window
let's try to draw sap from this long winter.
Spring has come losing his colors.

# MÉTODO PARA CALCULAR EL TIEMPO
*Daniel Calabrese, Argentina*

Los que viven a este lado de la ruta
saben de compensaciones:
cada vez que alguien pasa rumbo al Sur
anotan la hora exacta
y dejan caer una piedra en el vacío del ser.

Quienes viven del otro lado
conocen la polaridad:
cada vez que alguien pasa en sentido contrario,
de regreso,
anotan lo mismo,
pero sacan una piedra del vacío del ser.

Así unos llenan su vacío
y otros lo despejan.

Cada cierto tiempo,
los que han llenado su vacío
cruzan por el puente viejo (que era nuevo)
y esperan con paciencia
a que pasen los regresadores del Sur,
uno tras otro,
hasta que el vacío es total.

# METHOD FOR CALCULATING TIME
*Daniel Calabrese, Argentina*
*Translated by Katherine M. Hedeen, USA*

Those who live on this side of the route
know about compensation:
every time someone goes by headed toward the
South
they write down the exact time
and let a stone fall into the void of being.

Those who live on the other side
know polarity:
every time someone goes by the other way,
coming back,
they write it down too,
but they take a stone out of the void of being.

And so some fill their void
and others empty it.

After a while
those who've filled their void
cross the old bridge (which was new)
and patiently wait
for the returners from the South to go by,
one after another,
until the void is complete.

# LUCE PER GABBIANI
*Deborah D'Agostino, Italia*


Si schiude il cancello di luce.
Ignorato Orizzonte, scavo dentro.
Penelope nuova, tesso trame di speranze.
Gabbiani impazziti sul marmo del mondo.
Non vedi il porto? Rumore non c'è
che possa coprire il canto interiore.
Tra le vetrate i gabbiani hanno inventato il mare.

# LIGHT FOR SEAGULLS
*Deborah D'Agostino, Italy*
*Translated by Helen Guyatt, UK*

The gateway of light opens.
Horizon ignored, I look inside.
Penelope modern, weaving a hopeful plot.
Crazed seagulls on the marble of the world.
Do you not see the port? There is no noise
that can smother the inner song.
Among high windows the seagulls
have invented the sea.

## STRANGE DAYS
### *Don Krieger, USA*

*… one in a thousand black men [in America]*
*can expect to be killed by police …*
Edwards et al, Proceedings of the
National Academy of Science
116(34), 2019: 16793-16798

I woke to the governor's
stay-at-home order,
drove the turnpike anyway.
Each cop we passed,
and there were many,

I thought of my white Subaru,
and my skin,
like a thousand times before.

# WHEN WILL WE REAP THE WHIRLWIND?
*Don Krieger, USA*

*... 2020 ... deadliest year for*
*gun violence [in America]*
*... 43,500 ... deaths*
American Journal of Managed Care,
July 28, 2021

Billboards then:
Segregation now.
Segregation forever.
Visualize World Peace.

These days with the covid
we keep the windows shut
hold our water
drive like the hunted
like the dispossessed.

True Christians
obey Christ.
Women who serve
gain Paradise.

At the rest stop
every other face
exposed, guns at the ready,
the others with face masks
like targets.

# RĂZBOI
*Dorel Cosma, România*

Sântem  în tranşee.
E război!
Prin lupă
craniul  amăgirilor
continuă.
Străzi cocoşate
nu vedem
inamicul,
nu mai avem
gust.
Se trage
cu tunul,
mitraliere  restrictive.
Inamicul scapă.
Ne baricadăm
în case
căutăm în cărţi
şi rugă
cheia eliberării.
S-a spart
frontul.
Răbdarea
nu mai are
margini,
aranjăm dureri,
furie amestecată
cu frică
şi violenţa adevărului.
Oricând
poate suna
sirena,
ne adăpostim
cu mâini spălate
şi nu ne recunoaştem
în privirea inutilă
de sub  mască.

Războiul e război,
nu ştii
pe unde pătrunde
şi cine e duşmanul.
Spitalele sunt pline,
avem răniţi
avem şi morţi,
avem şi generalii
depăşiţi
de gustul mierii.
Mulţimea se revoltă,
Ecou pierdut
în norul zdrenţuit.
Sunt prea puţini !
Cu scuturi
Pfizer şi Azteca
începe apărarea.
Sub platoşa
fumului sufocant
generalii
spumegă
de glorie !
Cu funiile
legate de pat
muribunzii
scrâşnesc din dinţi.
Cine să-i audă?
În praful soarelui
cu răsuflarea umedă
vulgaritatea spionează,
duşmanul râde,
aristocraţia furtunii
decretează noi restricţii.
Noi : aplaudăm

## WAR

*Dorel Cosma, Romania*
*Translated by Zorin Diaconescu*

We're in the trenches.
It's war!
Through a magnifying glass
the skull of deceptions
keeps going.
Humped streets
we can't see
the enemy,
we don't have any more
taste.
He shoots
his cannon,
restrictive machine guns.
The enemy escapes.
We barricade ourselves
in houses
we look up in books
and pray
the key to liberation.
The front
broke up.
Patience
has no more
edges,
we arrange pain,
mixed anger
with fear
and the violence of truth.
whenever
the siren
 may sound,
we take shelter
with washed hands
and we don't recognize each other
in the useless look

from under the mask.
War is war,
you do not know
where it enters
and who is the enemy.
Hospitals are full,
we have wounded
we have the dead,
we also have the generals
exceeded
for the taste of honey.
The crowd revolts,
Lost echo
in the ragged cloud.
There are too few!
With shields
Pfizer and Azteca
the defense begins.
Under the plate
suffocating smoke
generals
foaming
of glory!
With ropes
related to the bed
dying
I grit my teeth.
Who can hear them?
In the dust of the sun
with wet breath
vulgarity spies,
the enemy laughs,
the aristocracy od storms
enacts new restrictions.
We: we applaud

# İŞARETLER
*Elçin Sevgi Suçin, Türkiye*


sesin olayım istiyorum senin
diline dolaşayım
ağzının şiirli çiçeği bilsinler beni.

tohumlar gibi kalbimde, kabarıyor
kıpırdanıyor etimdeki toprak.
çiçek mi açacak ne köşedeki ağaç
dudaklarımla aynı renk olmuş dalları.

bütün kış ikimizin de omuzlarında
siyah beyaz bir palto
içimize çekildik, o köklerini ben kendimi
bir devrime hazırlanır gibi sessiz, gayretli.

martın ilk günleriydi, önce kuşlar
sonra kedilerin aşk çığlıkları, uyandık
damarlarımızda yeşil bir kıpırtı
gerindik, gerindi toprak da bizimle.

ilkin çiğdemlerin toprağı yırtma sesi
vişne ağacının ilk çiçekleri sonra
ve kalbimden gül çıkaran ellerin
şiir gibi bir şey oldu, bahar gelmiş.

öyle dedi, bisiklete binen çocuklar.

# SIGNS
*Elçin Sevgi Suçin, Turkey*
*Translated by Neil P. Doherty, Ireland*

how I long to be your voice,
wrapped around your tongue
let them see me as the lyric flower of your mouth

like seeds swelling in my heart
the soil in my flesh stirs
the tree in the corner is about to bloom
its branches now the same hue as my lips.

a black and white coat draped over our shoulders
throughout the winter
we withdrew into ourselves, silent yet intent as if
he were readying his roots and I, myself for
revolution.

with birds and the love cries
of cats the first days of March arrived;
we awoke, a quivering of green in our veins.
we stretched out, the earth stretched out with us.

at first came the sound of the crocus tearing the earth
then, the early flowers of the cherry tree
and your hands plucking roses from my heart,
something poetic came to pass, spring is here,

or so the cycling children said

# KİRAZ ÇİÇEĞİ
### *Emel Koşar, Türkiye*

58

Seyyan Hanım'a

örtük hüsran
meyvesiz çiçek
ateşin öptüğü
rüzgârın kokladığı kalkan
bekledikçe koyulaşan nisan
küllendim
çöken geceyle
küllendim
nehirlerce
bana ışığı getiren kuzgun
dinlendirilmiş keder
yaraların yaralandığı
mimoza, ertelenmiş bahar
mazi kalbimde bir yaradır
bana bir ateş bahşet
sözlerin kıyamet

# CHERRY BLOSSOM
*Emel Koşar, Turkey*
*Translated by Yasemin Kurtuluş, Turkey*

to Miss Seyyan

uncovered frustration
blossom without fruit
shield which kissed by fire
which smelled by the wind
april, which getting darker as you wait
i got ashes over me
by the falling night
i got ashes over me
by the rivers
raven which brings me the light
sorrow has been rested
mimosa, which wounds
have wounded, deferred spring
past is a wound in my hearth
grant to me a fire
your words are apocalypse

## WER BIST DU?
*Emina Čabaravdić-Kamber,*
*Deutschland/Bosnien-Herzegowina*

Wer bist DU
Der in der Nacht
Den Schlaf raubt
Und
In der Morgendämmerung
Der Seele
Flügel verleiht

Wer bist DU
Der keinen Unterschied
Für seine Zeilen
Zwischen den Zeiten
Sucht
Sie
In Frühlingsblüten
Heißen Sommernächten
Zwischen Herbstblättern
Und
In Winterstürmen
Findet

Wer bis DU
der aus der Ferne
Nähe schafft
Und
Das Herz höher
Schlagen lässt

Wer bist DU
Der die Sehnsucht
In sich schreibt
Sie
In Kirschblüten
Aufleben lässt

Wer bist DU

## WHO ARE YOU ?

*Emina Čabaravdić-Kamber, Bosnia*
*Translated by Barry Stevenson,*
*United Kingdom*

Who are YOU
That steals sleep
In the night
And
At the day's dawning
Lends wings
To the soul


Who are YOU
That seeks no difference
For its lines
Between the seasons
She
Finds in the bloom of spring
In hot summer nights
Between the autumn leaves
And
The storms of winter


Who are YOU
That makes nearness
Out of distance
And
The heart
Beat stronger

Who are YOU
That writes yearning
Into the self
She
Has the cherry blossom
Come alive

Who are YOU

## Eski Konuk

*Erkut Tokman, Türkiye*


Sonsuz boşluklara yayılan,
Sessizliğin dilini yoğuran
Senle benim aramda
Evreni dolduran karanlık madde

Bir ütopya, toz bulutunda,
Bir düş, sancılı ruhumuzda gebe
Çağların zaman aralıklarında

Bir yaydan çıkan okla kalbimize saplanmış
Varoluş denklemine dayalı eksik hipotez,
Önlenemez değişim ve d/evrim.
Bir serzenişi var oysa yolculuğunda
Hayalini kurduğumuz dünyaların yokluğunda

Sonunda hep yeniden içeri davet ettiğin
İnsanlığın kapısına dayanmış o
En eski konuk; Yalnızlık
Aklının coğrafyasında kayıp bir rüzgâr şimdi,
Unutuşun ateşiyle kavrulan bir anı,
Hayat dediğin, ruh yangını
Bir türlü kaçıp kurtulamadığın

## AN OLD GUEST
*Erkut Tokman, Turkey*
*Translated by İdil Karacadağ, Turkey*

Embodying the mute language
dark matter merging universe
diffusing into infinite space,
between you and me

An utopia hidden therein dust cloud
a dream got pregnant aching within our souls,
bounded by milestones of the ages

Since incomplete hypothesis based on an equation of
existence
An arrow sprung from its bow targeted our hearts
Inescapable metaplasia of r-evolution
Yet it has a grievance
amongst the worlds that we imagine

In the end once again you have invited in
the one knocked at humanity's door
Is the oldest guest; Solitude!
A lost wind on the geography of your mind,
A memory scorched by the heat of forgetfulness
called life which you can't get away from
the flames of soul within.

# A DEVIL'S BARGAIN (Persephone's song)
*George Wallace, USA*

I was a child, I wore my hair in braids, flowers grew in
my footsteps, my mother loved me; it was always
spring & when it was not spring it was harvest, there
was grain & pumpkins & grapes purpling on the vine,
my mother was my harvest song & the people were
well fed & knew the deal;

until death came along & kissed me on the lips -- "I
will make you my queen" said death;

so I went home with death & ruled by death's side; &
flowers no longer grew in my footsteps & I no longer
braided my hair; & I sat on death's throne and
listened to the terrible, mighty songs only death
knows;

songs of the wicked, songs of the damned, songs of
the just plain ordinary dead; all the songs that lie
beyond the grave & give solace to the no longer
living; all the choruses of the damned which emanate
from hell's bloody mouth;

& I learned to love their songs, as a queen is meant to
do, & it was all okay, a devil's bargain;

my mother got in the way, that is, she was lonesome
and depressed; & before you could count the hairs on
hera's head, all the grapes withered on the vine; all
the grain turned to ashes in the mouths of the people
& all the crops blew away;
the harvest was ruined & the people suffered, they no
longer knew the difference between being alive &
dead; & the noise of the suffering was too much for
everybody -- more terrible than wind or snow or rain;

terrible to me
terrible to my mother
terrible to the ears of the gods;

& I no longer loved to hear death sing to me;

so now I spend six months of every year on earth,
braiding my hair, pretending to be my mother's child;
& I spend six months in hell in the arms of my spouse,
the great lord death, pretending to be his queen;
nobody's satisfied, everybody knows the deal;

everybody's depressed & down at the mouth
on earth as it is in hell
that's just the way death likes it.

## PEACE IS HONEY
### *George Wallace, USA*

Peace isn't the absence of war.
It is sweet milk in a clean bucket.
It is the bleating of goats in an honest
man's yard. Peace is the honking of geese
in the pond, cicadas chirping in the tall grass.
Peace is olive presses, wine presses,
harvesters clamoring for more fruit
in the foothills of the Lower Galilee.
More than silence of dawn with no rockets
to disturb it, peace is rooster crowing,
hen clucking -- plow points, shovels and
stiff rakes and hoes rattling in the back
of a pickup truck. It is the buzz of harvest
machines combing the harmonious land –
horizon to horizon, feeding all the
children women and men without
prejudice, giving all the people
in the land full employ.
Peace is Palestinian boys
in the apiaries of Doura,
west of Hebron, working
their father's hives. It is
a cloud of honeybees
hovering over the roof-
tops of Kibbutz
Ayelet Hashahar.
Peace is not just
the absence of
small arms fire,

or treaty-signing
ceremonies in
far away capitals.
It is more than just
who gets what,
who loses what,
and both sides
agree to accept it.
Peace is more than
the absence of war.

Peace is wild ducks splashing in the Jordan River.
Peace is the shared laughter of workers in the field.

Peace is honey and milk in the land of milk and
honey.

# DER DUFT DES LEBENS
*Gino Leineweber, Deutschland*


Keine Grenzen Begrenzung Generation

Der Wahnsinn
Verströmt
Vom Duft des Lebens
Beendet meine Tollheit
Ich atme jetzt
Die Gerüche des Herbstes
Der Wald ist schon in Sicht
Die Sonne die so lange schien
Ist verhüllt
Vom Duft der Bäume

Ich gehe weiter
Obwohl der Winter naht
Ich gehe hindurch

Es kommt ein anderer Frühling

# ODOR OF LIFE
*Gino Leineweber, Germany*


No borders no limits no age

The madness which is in
The odor of life
Has ceased my madness
I now inhale
Smells from the fall
The forest is already in sight
The sun that has shone so long
Appears only veiled
Behind the fragrance of trees

I am walking further
Though the winter is coming
I am going through

There is another spring

# BENİMLE DOLSUN
*Gülname Albayrak, Türkiye*


Dedi ki bana
Uzağız ama
Aynı mavi göğe bakıp
Aynı nefesi aldığımız için
Tanrıya şükrediyorum.
İşte o zaman
Güneşi koparıp kalbime soktu
Onunla doldum.
Bu bahar gelemez belki uzaktan
Ama ömrüme bahar getirdi
Okyanusun kokusunu,
Menekşelerin rengini,
Kuşların melodisini,
Erguvan ağaçlarının dansını
Ben de, onun için
Buradan bahar rüzgarlarına
Bir papatya bırakıyorum
Mavi gökyüzünde görsün diye
Benimle dolsun diye

# TO FİLL WİTH ME
*Gülname Albayrak, Turkey*
*Translated by Ian Sinclair, Scotland*

He said to me
We are far
But I thank God for looking at the same blue sky
And take the same breath
That's when
He plucked the sun
And put it in my heart
I'm filled with him
Maybe this Spring can't come from afar
But Spring has brought my life
The smell of the ocean,
The color of violets,
The melody of birds,
The dance of the redbud trees
Me too, for him
I leave a daisy to the Spring winds from here
To appear in the blue sky
To fill with me

இளவேனிற்காலம் வந்துவிட்டது ...
     ஹேமா ரவி, இந்தியா

மந்தமான குளிர்காலம் பின்னால் விடப்பட்டுள்ளது
பல வண்ண ஆடைகளில் அலங்கரிக்கப்பட்டிருக்கிறாள்
சூரியன் மற்றும் காற்றால் புத்துயிர் பெற்றாள்
புதிய உடையில் அவள் மயக்குகிறாள்.

பல வண்ண ஆடைகளில் அலங்கரிக்கப்பட்டிருக்கிறாள்
நீண்ட குளிர்  உணர்ச்சிகளை அடக்கி வைத்திருந்தது
புதிய உடையில் அவள் மயக்குகிறாள்
இனி வெறுமையாகவும், நிர்வாணமாகவும் இல்லை.

நீண்ட குளிர் உணர்ச்சிகளை அடக்கி வைத்திருந்தது
வாழ்க்கை இருட்டாகவும் மந்தமாகவும் ஆகியிருந்தது
இனி வெறுமையாகவும், நிர்வாணமாகவும் இல்லை
களைப்புற்ற கண்கள் இப்பொழுது மகிழ்ச்சியுடன்
பளபளக்கிறது.

வாழ்க்கை இருட்டாகவும் மந்தமாகவும் ஆகியிருந்தது
வருத்தம் இல்லாமல், அனைத்தையும் ஏற்றுக்கொண்டாள்
களைப்புற்ற கண்கள் இப்பொழுது மகிழ்ச்சியுடன்
பளபளக்கிறது
இப்பொழுது, அவள் உயரமாக நிற்க தயாராக இருக்கிறாள்.

வருத்தம் இல்லாமல், அனைத்தையும் ஏற்றுக்கொண்டாள்
சூரியன் மற்றும் காற்றால் புதுப்பிக்கப்பட்டது.
இப்பொழுது, அவள் உயரமாக நிற்க தயாராக இருக்கிறாள்
மந்தமான குளிர்காலம் பின்னால் விடப்பட்டுள்ளது.


74

# SPRING'S ARRIVED ...
### *Hema Ravi, India*

Dreary winter's been left behind
Adorned in multi-colored clothes
Revived by the sun and the wind
She mesmerizes in that pose.

Adorned in multi-colored clothes
For long, the chill had sedated.
She mesmerizes in that pose
No longer barren and naked!

For long, the chill had sedated
Life had become dark and dreary.
No longer barren and naked
Droopy eyes have become cheery.

Life had become dark and dreary
Without remorse, accepted all.
Droopy eyes have become cheery
Now, She's ready to stand up tall.

Without remorse, accepted all
Revived by the sun and the wind
Now, She's ready to stand up tall.
Dreary winter's been left behind.

# BURNU BÜYÜK BAHARLAR BALADı
*Hilal Karahan, Türkiye*

Uzun zaman oldu görüşmüyoruz erguvanlar ve
soluğunuz;
uzun zamandır sesinizi gökyüzünden tanıyoruz.

Itır kokusu, yasemin çayı, öğle vakti biliriz;
sade ve güneşli günleri seversiniz,
kapı önlerinde sessiz güler buluruz sizi,

—Gece gölge değildir
hırs, ihtar edilmiş hareket—

Koridorlarda yürürsünüz, pencere aralarında,
duvar diplerinde, eşiklerde,
Yeni uyanmış kırışıkları kuşlara yedirerek,
korktuğumuz yollardan döner sıkıntılı sesiniz:

— Bellek tehlikeli bir düzmece—

Üçgen bir kalabalıkta anımsarız sizi dalgın,
iç açıları ağrıyan bir dal erguvan,
çağın sertleşme sorununa teğet,
ayak fetişizmine dik bakan;

—Bilinçaltı çöplüğünde durmadan kurulan
ve dağılan kabarık insan—

Hiç anlamayız ama akla aldırmayız: aşıkken
kim tanıyabilir birbirini? Yeni giysilere alışır
gibi alışılır yeni aşka: biraz daha açık,
biraz daha kısa.

Gürültüyle anımsarız balkona oturunca gün üşümüş
burnunuz ve kırmızı kravatınız: kocaman burnunuz
ve sümüklü susarız salonun ortasında:

—Görülmenin anlamı yok—

Saçınıza dokunuruz usulca devrilir birbirine iki tren!
Yine elimizi yıkamadan, üzerinizi soyunmadan yine
yüzümüz cam.

Uzak bir limandan dönüyor olmalı bu kuşlar...

# THE BALLAD OF HAUGHTY SPRINGS
*Hilal Karahan, Turkey*

It has been long time since we saw each other, the
Judea trees and your breath;
for a long time we recognize your voice from the sky.

We, the scent of pelargonium, jasmine tea, the noon
time,
all know that you like simple, sunny days,
we find you laughing silently in front of the doors,

—The night is not a shadow
ambition, admonished movement—

You walk in the corridors, among the windows,
at the feet of walls, at the doorsteps,
By making birds to eat recently awakened wrinkles
your worried voice turns back the roads that frighten
us:

—The memory is a dangerous forgery—

In a triangular crowd we remember you, pensive
a Judean tree branch, whose inner angles are hurting
who looks tangentially to the age's erection disorder,
perpendicularly to foot fetishism;

—Man is a transient swelling in the subconscious
dump,
which is constantly being built and dispersed—

We never understand yet we don't care the mind:
who can know one another while we are in love?
We get used to new love as we get used to new
clothes:
little looser, little shorter.

Once the day sits in the balcony
we, your cold nose and red tie remember noisily:
we, your big and snotty nose, sit quietly in the middle
of the room:

—No meaning to be seen—

We touch your hair gently two trains tilt over each
other!
Again, without washing our hands, you still without
undressing,
our face is glass.
These birds must be returning from a remote port.

FLEDGLING
  *Holly Iglesias, USA*

*resounding/anew, anew*
(Lorine Niedecker, *If I were a bird*)

Fourteen, hungry to ponder deep things, lofty things, I grabbed a volume from my mother's bookcase on Saturday mornings—Sonnets from the Portuguese, Harvard Classics, Volume 5: Essays, Emerson—and sat on the violet-bedecked embankment along the Missouri-Pacific Railroad tracks to read and reflect, what the nuns called lectio divina, except not contemplating the divine but the mortal, for I was happily earthbound, drunk with corporeal life, and vowed to turn my attention to Beauty, Remorse, Passion, Death, wondering all the while if thinking such thoughts was Philosophy—or Poetry. One thing was certain: my body was changing by leaps and bounds and my mind wanted that too, to consume a rich diet of paperbacks bought with my own money—Modern European Poetry, What Is Existentialism? The Federalist Papers—the entire experience transforming, from perusal to purchase to the slow walk home, swinging the paper bag like a boulevardier. Ah, thought I—noting the predicate before the subject, sensing a trinity of exclamatory sentences about to burst from me—Ah, Philosophy! Ah, Poetry! Ah, Europe!

# FALSE SPRING, OHIO, 1970
*Holly Iglesias, USA*



*Rough winds do shake the darling buds of May,*
*And summer's lease hath all too short a date.*
(William Shakespeare)

Picture a girl in a macramé vest walking to class
against a backdrop of barely budding trees, another
with untamed hair, rocks in her pockets, and some
boys in T-shirts, some in button-downs, impromptu
flags in their fists. Their brief past already points to
this moment—little girls in Sunday dresses blown to
bits in Birmingham, a boy dredged from a Mississippi
swamp, on the skirt of a pink Chanel suit a stain
shaped like a map of the future— lunchtime in
America, another grassy knoll. Thirteen seconds,
sixty-seven rounds, and the pool of dreams begins to
drain as a head hits concrete, as legs buckle, as
shoes stumble over themselves, the camera
capturing a girl kneeling beside a body on the
ground, her mouth enormous, the body's life leaching
into the earth, the season passing well before its time.

SINOPEM
  *hülya n. yılmaz, Turkey/USA*

En ufak köşesini bile düşlüyorum bu sıralar
memleketin;
o eşsiz kokusu her hücremde, buram buram.
Susamışım inanılmaz.
Doyulacak gibi bir açlık değil bu.
Hasreti dağlamış özünü dimağımın.

Çocukluğum geçti birçok kalp atışında,
hele ki gençliğimin o kaygısız ön yılları;
ilk yetişkinliğimin en ulu cazibesi de orada.
Unutamam ne yaşadıklarımı ne de umduklarımı.

Şirin şipşirin bir yeri yokluyor nabzımı vatanın
sık sık.
Denizle kucaklaşmış o bir masal kitabı gibi şehir.

İşte o güzelim rıhtım karşıda,
çay bahçelerine bakıyor;
can dayımın öğretisi dondurma revanili café ise
sağda,
iç kıyıdaki hapisane kulesine dürbünle nöbet tutuyor.
Az ötede ada . . . patikası ip incesi,
bir çocuklar bayramı korteji sanki,
ara sokaklardaki hanelerle birlik olmuş coşuyor;
her birinden müzik yüklü yaşantılarımı topluyor.

Ada yolunu izliyorum;
beni en yüksek noktasına götürüyor şehrin;
deniz tüm heybeti ve canlılığıyla göz önünde,
sere serpe.

İşte karşımda duruyor o ev,
çocukluğumun tüm esrarıyla.
Biraz benzi atmış boyasının,
gene de şatafatlı, o şehrin denizi kadar.
Tarifsiz bir şefkat kokuyor
üzerine yayıldığı toprağında.
Pencereler iyice göğe doğru uzanmış sanki,
artık içini ısıtamayan can varlıklarım gibi.

Annemi algılıyorum merdivenlerinde o evin.
Genç. Hayat fışkırıyor her halinden.
Bir o kadar da güleç.
Bir de elimdeki geçmişe bakıyorum . . .

Küçücük bir çocuk o birden,
annesi yanında, pencereden babasını izliyor;
elinde çanta başında pek yakışan
geniş kenarlı bir şapka;
yanındaki çocuk o bambaşka can yakınım.
Anneannemi pek seçemiyorum – karanlıkta kalmış.
Annem yanında, dedim, ama peki ya
kucağındaki bebek? O da karanlıkta.
Tamam, tanıdım. Pek az tadabildiğim
o çocuktan hasta diğer can varlığım.
Yanıbaşımda annemin kokusu,
kalbinin sımsıcaklığı . . .

Kah yürüyorum dar ve dik yokuşlarında o şehrin;
kah dalmış çocuk gözlerim denizine uçsuz bucaksız.
Benliğimin özünde yaşanmışlıkların
yaşanamamışlıkların ağırlığı,
yaşanabileceklerin endişesi hem de meraklı bekleyişi.
Bir de şu toprağını içlemesi yok mu
şu gurbet ağacının!

Bahara gözyaşları içinde dalları.
Uzun sürdü kış bu sefer,
güneşine yanık ana vatanın, ve de içe çekilesi
havasına.

Yanıbaşımda annemin kokusu,
kalbinin sımsıcaklığı . . .

# MY BELOVED SINOP
### *hülya n. yılmaz, Turkey/USA*

the homeland enters the main vein
her scent floods to each body cell
one stunning aroma after another . . .
i thirst in hunger pangs

etched to memory in blood and flesh,
emerges the magic of my early life
often asleep – the head should feel sore
however, when awake, it aches no more
"snow falls upon those who sleep", she whispers . . .
the blanket over me is soaked in her perfume
my pillow is filled with the softest feathers

one corner – a distinctive delight
a town in unison with its sea
unlocks the long suppressed

there!
it stretches to the harbor in cheer
the main street is dressed in tea gardens of
yesteryear
Divan café – as loyal as ever before
hugs the aged salt factory
affectionately mends its bruises
right before the old prison, it is guarded
by the compliant inner bay
not at all anxious by its fast-descending bend
sates every passer-by with secrets-devouring treats
my childhood eyes and arousing sighs
on loads and loads of mouth-watering plates
a huge piece of Revani – apt for my sweet-tooth-fame
topped with natural ice cream of vanilla beans

delights generation after generation after generation
eight in total, the loved ones of mine

farther away lies the town's aorta
the legendary passage to the famed Ada
coveting April 23rd parades of ribbon bouquets
on Çocuk Bayramı – The Festival of Children . . .
and flows in sync with streets wide open
alleys unseen
carrying along a dear one of mine
to the heart's mind scene by scene


my eyes are locked on the trail to the highest peak
one modest look to the left or the right
the sea struts its azure wealth and might


and there, a mere breath away
dons its mysteries that spectacular house
bricks worn out shutters in ashen hue
still erect in humility though
vies few more breaths to accrue
ornate transoms eye the vastness of the sky
their weathered glances cast down upon the sea
the soil tender as a new mother's caress
depleted tree roots soon to finally rest
as have those who were put there abreast

my heart wanders off to the faded print in my hand:
wide steps to a wooden tall entry door
a stately man – fedora briefcase handsome face
my uncle by his leg – a mere toddler
a Shirley Temple, though Turkish, my mother
her small gleaming face ever so bright
glued to the colossal front window

my grandmother's beauty re-appears in the dark
tucked in on her lap, my other uncle – her youngest
whose cruel damaged pre-natal heart
cut off too soon his contagious delight

next to me
the unique scent of my mother
the warmest warmth of her soul

# ХАВРЫН ТЭР МОДОНД БИ ДУРЛАЧИХЛАА

*Жэнни Лхагвасурэн, Монгол*

Тэнгэрийн рашааны мөнгөн дусалд
Хаврын навчис уусан цэнгэхэд
Өнгө жавхаа нь гайхалтайяа тодорно
Үүнийг гүйцэх өнгө байна уу
Дурлачихлаа, байгалийн тэр ногоон өнгөнд
Дурлачихлаа, байгалийн тэр уран хийцэнд

Бүжих салхины зүггүй илбээнд
Навчис хөөрөн уяран сэржигнэхэд
Гоо үзэсгэлэн нь улам төгөлдөржинө
Үүнийг гүйцэх үзэсгэлэн байна уу
Дурлачихлаа, байгалийн тэр төгс зохицолд
Дурлачихлаа, нов ногоон нахиатай тэр модонд

# I FELL IN LOVE WITH THAT SPRING TREE
*Jenny Lkhagvasuren, Mongolia*


The spring leaves rejoice at the silver drops from
celestial water
The scenery looks better than ever
There is no such attractive thing as this
It is beyond my comparison
I fell in love with the natural green color
I fell in love with the natural art

The spring leaves rustle sentimentally
In the dancing and wild wind
It brings forth the most beautiful form
There is no such lovely thing as this
It is beyond my comparison
I fell in love with the natural perfect harmony
I fell in love with the tree with totally green leaves

# PRIMAVERA AZUL

*Juan C. Tajes,*
*Uruguay/Holanda*

En aquel ayer contaba
Con los años primaveras
Y una cinta era el tiempo
De azules tardes ligeras,
Colgadas de rama en rama
Al árbol de mis deseos.

También sumaban los días
Peripecias y recuerdos,
Acrobáticos abrazos
Con gestos torpes, ligeros,
Horas de besos salados
En la playa de otros cuerpos.

Fui copero de los dioses.
Fui dardo, agua y espejo.
Fui ala, fui roca y bosque.
Fui abismo, horizonte y fuego.
Ahora entreveo las sombras
En esta orilla del sueño.

Ya no soy yo, soy el otro
En la cinta azul del tiempo.

# BLUE SPRING
### *Juan C. Tajes, Uruguay/The Netherlands*

In that yesterday I counted
Over the years the springs
And a ribbon was the time
Of light blue afternoons,
Hanging from branch to branch
To the tree of my desires.

I also added the days
Adventures and memories,
Of acrobatic hugs
With clumsy, light gestures,
Hours of kisses and sea salt
On the beach of other bodies.

I was cupbearer of the gods.
I was dart, water and mirror.
I was wing and rock and forest.
I was abyss, horizon and fire.
Now I only glimpse the shadows
from this shore of the dream.

I am no longer me, I am the other
On the blue ribbon of time.

# AQUELLA PRIMAVERA
*Julio Pavanetti, Uruguay/España*


Desde dentro me asaltan los recuerdos
como lluvia que nace en el pasado
y no envejece. Vuelven indecisos
como los árboles, como los pájaros,
por los márgenes de una primavera
adelantada, lista para el cambio,
desperezada, abierta en filamentos
plateados que crecen como el llanto.

Imprudente, me brota en la memoria
aquella primavera, recordándome
cómo nació mi amor... entre sus brazos.

# THAT SPRING
### *Julio Pavanetti, Uruguay/Spain*


From within I am assailed
by memories, like rain that is born
in the past and does not age.
They come back undecided
like trees, like birds,
by the margins of an early spring,
ready for change, stretched,
open in silver filaments
that grow like tears.

Reckless, springs in my memory
that spring, reminding me
how my love was born ... in her arms.

ΠΑΤΡΙΚΌ ΈΔΑΦΟΣ
*Λιάνα Σακελλίου, Ελλάδα*

Ο Μαραθώνας είναι αρχαία πόλη
σχεδόν Ηλύσια, λέω
καθώς σκαρφαλώνουμε τον λόφο
που περιέχει τους νεκρούς.
Παντού αλατισμένοι βολβοί που γίνονται σαφράνια.
Ο τάφος είναι εδώ, λευκός σαν κόκαλο.
Η θάλασσα στο μπλε του κοβαλτίου.
Η μέρα γυμνή.

Μάραθος σημαίνει ρίζα, λέω
καθώς μαζεύουμε την πράσινη ρίζα
για να τη βάλουμε στο φαγητό–
ευωδιαστό ξόρκι.
Πόσο γρήγορα τα πράγματα ξεχνιόνται
χάνουνε σχήμα
χάνουνε όνομα
γίνονται κάτι άλλο.

Λέξεις στο στόμα
αντί για κραυγές
στη διάβρωση τόσων πολλών ερωτήσεων:
Ναι, πέρασες το σημείο ελέγχου.
Όχι, δεν είχες διαβατήριο.
Όχι, δεν ήσουν ενήλικας.
Τραύλιζες όταν μιλούσες.
Παραπατούσες όταν περπάταγες.

Κατάλαβες λάθος τις οδηγίες.
Εμπιστεύτηκες το μυστικό στα αδέρφια σου–
αυτά σε είχαν άλλωστε κρατήσει ζωντανό.
Ήσουν ανίκανος να ταξιδέψεις.

Δανείστηκες τη λέμβο τους.
Επανάλαβε την εκδοχή σου!
Ο ακτοφύλακας σε διέταξε
σαν μετρονόμος.

Τώρα το φως καίει
τιμωρητικό σαν το χιόνι.
Για μένα είναι άνοιγμα φτερών.
Για σένα καταρρέει στην άνοιξη σου
σαν μια βαριά κατασκευή.

# HOME
*Liana Sakelliou, Greece*

Marathon is an ancient city.
Almost Elysian, I say
as we crest the hill
that contains the dead.
Everywhere salted bulbs growing into crocuses.
The tomb is here, white as bone.
The day is naked.
The sea is cobalt on blue.
Marathos means root, I say
as we collect this root to
put into food— a green spell.

How fast things are forgotten
they lose shape
they lose name
they become something else.
Words in the mouth
instead of screams
at the elision of
so many questions:
Yes, you passed the checkpoint.
No, you did not have a passport.
No, you were not an adult.

You lisped as you talked.
You sidled as you walked.
You misheard instructions.
You consigned the secret to your brothers—
they had kept you alive after all.
You were unfit to travel.

You borrowed their raft.
Repeat your version!
The coast guard ordered
like a metronome.

Now the light is burning in
punishing as snow.
With me it' s a wingspan.
For you it collapses into your spring
like a heavy structure.

## ΠΑΡΑΔΟΞΟΤΗΤΕΣ
*Λιλυ Εξαρχοπουλου, Ελλαδα*

«Η άνοιξη μας έφτασε, εμπρός βήμα ταχύ
Να την καλωσορίσουμε παιδιά στην εξοχή»


Μάθαμε να σε συνδέουμε με την ύπαιθρο
Τις φυλλωσιές, τα έντονα χρώματα, τον ίμερο
Την προετοιμασία του ήλιου για την ωμότητα

Μάθαμε να σε συνδέουμε με ένα καλύτερο αύριο
Όπου όλα θα είναι ρόδινα- στο χρώμα σου-
Κι ας πρόκειται για μεταμφίεση οδοφραγμάτων

Να σε βλέπουμε σαν υπενθύμιση της θάλασσας
Μεγάλωμα της μέρας κι άνοιγμα του ζωτικού χώρου
Ένα παραμύθι αγρύπνιας και τολμηρών σχεδίων

Μάθαμε να ζωγραφίζουμε τα λουλούδια ακριβοδίκαια
Μόνο και μόνο γιατί πρόκειται για μυροβόλα παιδιά
σου
Γράψαμε ύμνους, τραγούδια, τροπάρια, συμφωνίες

Μας εγκατέλειψες άστοργα
Κλειστήκαμε σε οικήματα ψηλά κι απόρθητα
Εδώ ο υπολογιστής, τα μικροκύματα, η τηλεόραση
Το λίγο χώμα στην μαραγκιασμένη γλάστρα του
μπαλκονιού
Πιο κει ο ακάλυπτος, η μπουγάδα του απέναντι, οι
κεραίες

Μαραζώσαμε

Μετά ήρθε ο covid και μας αποτελείωσε
Χαίρε, ω χαίρε μάταιο έαρ του εγκλεισμού!

ODDITIES
*Lily Exarchopoulou, Greece*

"Spring has reached us in a great hurry
Come on kids, Let's meet her in the country"
(Greek Kindergarten Song)


We've learned to associate you with the countryside.
The foliage, the bright colors, the concupiscence,
Ardently preparing the sun for brutality

We've learned to connect you to a better tomorrow.
Where everything will be rosy - your color-
Even if you barricade in disguise.

We think of you as a reminder of the sea
Days become longer and spaces widen
Tales of awakening and daring future plans

We've learned to paint flowers fairly and justly
Just because they're your scented offspring
We wrote hymns, chants, songs, symphonies

You uncaringly abandoned us
We're locked up in houses high and impregnable.
Here the computer, the microwave, the TV
A little soil in the withered pot on the balcony
The skylight, the laundry across the street, the
antennae.

We're wilting away.

Then covid came and we were overcome
Hail, oh hail futile spring of seclusion!

# SIN NOSOTROS
*Luz Stella Mejía, Colombia/Estados Unidos*


Te perdono, primavera
por florecer en mi puerta sin preguntarme.
¿No te das cuenta, acaso
que aún estoy hibernando?
Haces que el cardenal exhiba impúdico
su color feliz en mi ventana
Afuera, el dulce canto de los vivos
saltando entre la hierba me excluye doloroso.

La vida desbordada en los jardines
me sorprende.
¿Cómo puedes ser tan bella
cuando somos rehenes del descuido?
Éramos hermanas en el tiempo
ahora tú vas por ahí regando flores
y yo hoy no soy parte del milagro.

Sospecho que lo sabes y desdeñas
Tal vez quieres decirnos algo
Tal vez quieren tú y la madre Tierra
celebrar nuestro encierro en una fiesta.

# WITHOUT US
### *Luz Stella Mejia, Colombia/USA*

I forgive you, Spring,
for blooming at my door
without my saying.
Perhaps you don't realize
that I'm still hibernating.
You make the cardinal display shameless
its happy color at my window
Outside, the sweet song of the living
jumping through the grass
excludes me painfully.

Life, overflowing in the gardens,
surprises me.
How can you be so beautiful
when I am hostage to carelessness?
We were sisters in time
now you go around spilling flowers
and today I am not part of the miracle.

I suspect that you know it and disdain it
Maybe you want to tell us something
Maybe you and Mother Earth finally want to
celebrate our confinement with a party.

ಅಗಳಿ ತಟ್ಟಿದ ಸದ್ದು
ಮಮತಾ ಸಾಗರ , ಭಾರತ


ಅಗಳಿ ತಟ್ಟಿದ ಸದ್ದು,
ಹೊರಗೂ... ಒಳಗೂ...
ಈಚೆಯಿಂದ ತೆರೆವ ಬಾಗಿಲ ಆಚೆಯಿಂದ ತಳ್ಳಿ
ಒಳನ್ನುಗ್ಗಿದ ಕತ್ತಲು ಬೆಳಕ ಬೀದಿಗೆಳೆದು
ರಸ್ತೆ ತುಂಬಾ ರಾದ್ಧಾಂತ...

ಒಳಹೊರಗೂ ಕತ್ತಲು ತುಂಬಿದಾಗ
ಕಮ್ಮಗೆ ಕಂಬಳಿ ಹೊದ್ದು ಮಲಗಿದವರಿಗೆ
ಕತ್ತಲ ಕೌದಿಯಡಿ ಹರಿವ ನೆತ್ತರ ಬಣ್ಣ ಕಾಣುವುದೇಯಿಲ್ಲ

ಆಗಾಗ ಕೇಳುತ್ತಿದ್ದ ಅಗಳಿ ತಟ್ಟಿದ ಸದ್ದು
ಈಗ ಎಲ್ಲೆಲ್ಲೂ ಕೇಳುತ್ತಿದೆ!

# KNOCK ON THE DOOR
*Mamta Sagar, India*

Knock on the door
from outside, from inside
Doors that open from this side are
thrust forcefully from that side.
Darkness barges in,
drags the lights out to the streets
anarchy, turmoil, an utter chaos…

when the dark spreads the inside out;
those that sleep under their cozy
concealed blankets
never see the RED of the blood
seeping under their dark sheaths

knocks, not so frequent
are now heard often from every side!

# NACH DEM WINTER
*Maren Schönfeld, Deutschland*


Wie eilt der Wegrand an mir vorbei
rennen Tulpen und Magnolien
es treibt mich voran
dich zu finden

Doch du bist schon da
die ganze Zeit läufst du stumm
neben mir her bis ich schließlich
eine Pause brauche

Du erwartest mich
auf der Bank unter der Birke
legst mir behutsam ein Tuch
aus Vogelgesang um

Die Tulpen bleiben stehen
leichter Wind geht durch den Baum
ich schließe die Augen
meine Gedanken werden leiser

Dann endlich höre ich
deine Worte

## WINTER'S END
*Maren Schönfeld, Germany*
*Translated by Barry Stevenson,*
*United Kingdom*

The edge of the headlong path
with it tulips and magnolias racing past me
drives me on and on
till I find you

But you are already here
all the time running mutely
by my side till finally
I need a break

You are waiting for me
on the bench under the birch tree
and gently lay a cloth
of birdsong all around me

The tulips stand still
a soft wind goes through the tree
I close my eyes
my thoughts become quieter

Then at last I hear
your words

## LENTE BLUES
*Marian Eikelhof, Nederland*

Och ja, mijn verlorene,
Het was een erg lange winter
We hadden nauwelijks voldoende kleding
om ons verdriet te bedekken
alles wat we deden was onderhandelen
met de dood
konden we maar een deal maken
dat ze mij meenam
niet jou.

Wat is het moeilijk om de eerste bloesemboom te
    zien
door al mijn tranen
de geur ruiken van pijn, gemis,
wanhoop.

Herinner je…
Jij en ik
We konden goed met elkaar overweg
David Bowie,
eerste sigaret, stiekem in de garage,
en urenlang badminton.

Ik neem je op mijn schouders,
Je bent zo zwak nu, zo fragiel.
Doet er niet toe
we zien de eerste bloesemboom
samen
jij en ik
en eindelijk
wordt het lente.

# SPRINGTIME BLUES
*Marian Eikelhof, The Netherlands*

Oh yes, my lost one,
It has been such a long winter
We had barely enough clothes
to cover up for all the sadness we felt
all we did was negotiate
with death
wish we could make a deal
please don't take him
take me.

Hard to see the first blossom tree
through all my tears
hard to smell
the fragrance in the air
filled with grief,
despair.

Do you remember..
you and I,
we really got along,
David Bowie,
first ciggy, sneaking into the barn,
hours and hours of badminton.

I'll take you on my shoulders
you are so weak now, so fragile.
Never mind,
we will see the first blossom tree
together, you and I,
and at last
it will be finally
springtime.

# EN GÜZEL ÇALIGÜLÜ
*Mesut Şenol, Türkiye*


Görünüşü ne kadar da çekici
Yaprakları gizliyor bir cenneti
Kutsal göklerin katları sanki
Hazır davet etmeye bir şölene seni
Uçurmaya sihirli bir halı üstünde

Karışıyor çiğler bir anda
Kar beyazı terle
Kaçamak dokunmalar sıcaklığı hissediyor
Çalıgülü kaslarını geriyor
Mutluluk kapısını açmaya

Coşku içinde yakalanmış ve tutsak
Bir duygunun doruğunda adı zevk
Uzun süre tutamazsınız onu orada
Çünkü artık siz kendiniz değilsinizdir
O özel anın geldiğini takdir etmek
Tek seçiminizdir

Çalıgülü'ne aşırı düşkünlük önemli bir konudur artık
Sürekli ve şiddetli bir arzuya dönmeye aday olarak.

# THE FINEST PRIMROSE
*Mesut Şenol, Turkey*


So appealing in appearance
Its petals hide a heaven
Layers of those divine skies
Ready to invite you to a feast
To fly you on a magical carpet

In an instant the dew mixes
With the snowy sweat
The robbing touches feel the heat
The primrose flexes its muscles
To open up the gate of happiness

Caught and imprisoned in an excitement
Equal to the climax of a pleasing sentiment
Then you could not hold it in a long time
Where you cannot be yourself anymore
You would have no choice but to appreciate
That the special moment has arrived

An extreme fondness for the primrose becomes an
issue
A candidate to become a constantly burning desire.

# PRENZLAUER BERGFRÜHLING
*Michael Speier, Deutschland*


die pfiffe pasternaks
am wasserturm

samt fließt aus boxen
bodies bolschewicken

alle reisen sind spiegel
: frühlingsblind

drei junge platanen
im stützkorsett

– die wände?
eckige labyrinthchen

# SPRING IN EAST BERLIN
*Michael Speier, Germany*
*Translated by Richard Dove, Germany*

pasternaks`s whistles
from the watertower

velvet is flowing from boxes
bodies are bolsheviking

all journeys are mirrors
: springblind

three young plane trees
trussed up in supportive corsets

– the walls?
angular labyrinthlets

## НЕДЕЉА ЈЕ
*Милица Јефтимијевић Лилић, Србија*

Једногласан наступ птица и цврчака
 Засењује сирене, буку велеграда.
Пратим га из празног парка.
 Не омета га одсуство публике и аплауза.
Пева се најискреније за себе.

 Запажам да рајски тренутак
Непредвиђеног концерта
 У сто птичјих гласова
 Може да исцели милионе.
Све оне што нису погнули главе
 Ни предали се безнађу
И нису притиснути глађу
Нити понижени,
Пред собом оптужени,
 За погрешне кораке и изборе,
Ни принуђени да јавно клече
 Како би дотакли стопе владара,
Ко и сви робови.

Овде се учи слободном дисању,
Певању на слободне теме,
 Лет у висине.

Све може да сачека,
Рокови за разводе,
Парнице, одмазде.

Недељно је јутро.
Литургијски звук птичје молитве
Окрепљује.
 Деца су уз мајчино крило.
Очеви листају дневне новине.
Разговор старица што допире
 Из отворених прозора, тих је
 И  без набоја свакодневих.

 Нико није заплакао,
Потрчао, опсовао.

 Недеља је,
Свето пролеће.

## IT IS SUNDAY
*Milica Jeftimijević Lilić, Serbia*
*Translated by Lazar Macura, Serbia*

The unanimous performance of birds and cicadas
Overshadows sirens, the noise of a metropolis.
I attend it from an empty park.
It is not hampered by the absence of audience or
applause.
The singing is so sincere.

I detect that the celestial moment
Of the unexpected concert
In one hundred birds' voices
Can heal millions of people.
All those who have not bowed their heads
Or surrendered to hopelessness
Who are not oppressed by hunger
Or humiliated,
Accused before themselves
For the wrong steps or choices,
Who are not forced to kneel publicly
In order to touch the ruler's feet
Like all slaves.

Free breathing is taught here,
Singing on free topics,
Flying high.

Everything may wait,
Terms of divorces,
Lawsuits, retaliations.

It is Sunday morning.
The liturgical sound of birds' prayer
Is refreshing.
Children are on their mothers' laps.
Fathers are turning the pages of dailies.
The conversation of old women coming
Through open windows is quiet
And without everyday tensions.

Nobody is weeping,
Running or swearing.

It is Sunday-
Holy Spring!

## TUTAMADIM

*Muberra Karamanoglu, Türkiye*

Sevdayı tutamadım.
Gitmelerin kadınıyım
Kah kara trenle giderim
Raylar kıvrılır ovalarda, dağlarda
Yalnızlık istasyonlarında açar gözlerimi
Hüzün kasabalarına bakarım
İnsanlar geçer kompartman önünden
Bebek ağlamaları işler geceye
Mahmur gözlerde isyan
Dörde bölünmüş uyku kaç eder?
Geceler aritmetik bilmez
Homurtuyla kalkar tren
Camdan bir kendime
bir de ovalara bakarım
Beni görür
Geceyi görür
Seni gözkapaklarımın altına atarım
Sevdayı tutamadım.
Gitmelerin kadınıyım
Kah otobüsle giderim
Terminalde vurur beni ayrıklığım
Bir kurşun geçer
Menzilde ben
Kimseler görmeden
yaramı suya tutarım
Muavin bağırır:
"Yoksun yolların
yoksul yolcusu kalmasın!"
Ne bir gözyaşı
ne de sallanan eller vardır yola çıkarken

Vedamı usulca
terminale bırakırım
Kıraç topraklarda rastlarım kendime
Ben ki kimsesiz bozkır ağacı
Soyunurum güneşe,
rüzgara ve sensizliğe
Bedenimle barışırım.

# I COULD NOT CLING
*Muberra Karamanoglu, Turkey*

I couldn't cling love.
I'm the woman who goes
Either by a black train
While the rails are curls
in the meadows or the mountains
I open my eyes to the station of loneliness
Looking at the towns of sadness
People pass in front of compartments
Cries of babies woven into the night
Riot in the sleepy eyes
How many if sleeps divided into four?
Nights do not know arithmetic
The train takes off with a growl
I look at myself from windows
and the meadow
It sees me
and the night
I'll toss you under my eyelids
I couldn't cling love.
I'm the woman who goes
Either by bus
Separation hits me in the terminal
A bullet passes
me in range
Without anyone seeing
I hold my wound under water
Deputy clerk shouts;
"Do not leave the destitute road's poor passengers
back!"
Either a tear

Nor are there waving hands on the way
I leave my farewell softly to the terminal
I meet myself in barren lands
I am a lonley steppe tree
I undress towards the sun,
to the wind,
to your absentee
Make peace with my body.

# GÖK YERLEŞMİŞ GÖLE
*Nurduran Duman, Türkiye*

gök yerleşmiş göle, bulutlar uçan halı
adımladık adımlıyoruz ayı, yürüyüşünü
üstünden geçiyoruz dansının, suyla zamanın


uçuşarak hidrojen etekleri süzülüyor
yanımızdan başımızdan. tan.
saçıp saçılarak tarçından maviye elmastan arıdan
tarlalar bahçeler beziyoruz yerin ipeğine


öğreniyoruz biz de ekip biçmeyi: ışığı

# THE SKY SETTLED ON THE LAKE
*Nurduran Duman, Turkey*
*Translated by Andrew Wessels, USA*

the sky settled on the lake, clouds a flying carpet
we prepare to step on the moon, its walk
and pass over the moon's dance, its water and time

rustling hydrogen skirts float
passing by our sides by our heads. daybreak.
we spread and are spread from cinnamon to blue
from diamond from bee
we're graced with fields and gardens on the earth's
silk

we, too, are learning to cultivate: its light

वसंत काल

पद्मजा अय्यंगार-पैडी, भारत

वसंत के फूलों की सुगन्ध
हवा में कुछ ऐसे महकती है
कि उदासी दूर हो जाती है
और, दुख और चिंताएं भी

विशाल, खुला, नीला आकाश
और उड़ते हुए आज़ाद पंछी
दे संकेत वसंत के आगमन का
और प्रकृति के पुनःप्रवर्तन का

करती हूँ मैं महसूस
आलिंगन की तरह
रजाई में महफ़ूस
खटमल की तरह

लगता है मैं हूँ लिपटी
और पूरी तरह से घिरी
वसंत के नीले रिबन में
जो है मेरा प्रिय रंग भी

## SPRING TIME
### *Padmaja Iyengar-Paddy, India*

Scent of spring blooms
wafts through the air
that dispels the gloom,
and all worries and care

The vast, clear blue sky
And birds that freely fly
signal spring's arrival
And nature's revival

Like a hug
I feel snug
Like a bug
in a rug

I feel wrapped
Totally enveloped
By the spring's ribbon blue
That's also my favorite hue

بشارة
رائد أنيس الجشي – السعودية


أنَا أُبشِّرُ بحلوى الموتِ
وأَدفنُ ضَحكي كغرابٍ حنونٍ
فيْ ألواحِ الرمل

الموتُ يمتصُ
الشحنةَ المنشّطةَ
لإعاقةِ أمنية

تَصادماتُ الحلم لا تُثمرُ
بدون خصوبة
والموت هو الخصوبة الفاعلة

هو المُحرِّضُ الوقتي
والفرصة التي لا تَتكرر

وحده الموتُ
لا يَنتهي بالموتِ
ولا يبدأ بالحياة

أنا أبشِّر بموتٍ حميدٍ
وطموحٍ حميدٍ
واستغناءٍ يَقتلُ الطموحَ المحدودَ
بانتفاء هوس البحث

استغناءٌ يَصنعُ مجدَه ببطء نحّاتٍ
فيْ صحيفة الأزلِ المائعة

...

## TIDINGS
*Raed Anis Al-Jishi, Saudi Arabia*


I bring you glad tidings of death's sweetness,
and bury my laughter as a soulful crow.

Death absorbs the activated charge
for a wish's obstruction.

The dream's implications are not effective
 without fertility.

Death is an active fertility.
It is the temporary motivation,
an opportunity that won't be repeated.
Only death doesn't end with death
and begin with life.

I bring you tidings of a Praiseworthy death,
and a Praiseworthy ambition,

and a resignation that kills
the limited ambition
by the abiosis of the obsession of seeking,
a resignation that makes its glory
as slow as a sculptor
on the liquid scriptures of eternity.

...

rugido de jaguara
*Raquel Martínez-Gómez, España*

la voz interna ruge
me asusta la prolijidad del poema
con su promesa de salvación

sé que no hay nada parecido
quizás solo un momento fugaz de calma
el placer de contemplar lo bello

se abre y cierra
y siempre acaba

igual me aferro a saciar la sed
como la loca que soy
prendida a ese instante que se marchita
que presiento punzante en el futuro

hay algo que ya no es nuevo…

la experiencia
    EXPERIENCIA

añadió infinito cuando hubo una primera vez
no cabía anticipar lo que acababa
parecía que el goce sería para siempre


la voz interna ruge
y sé que no cura el amargor
acaso recrea esa búsqueda
que da tumbos de ciega
    …la tarde es engullida por otro anochecer

quizás la voz me esté diciendo algo
midiendo en una escala
la infinitud de una estancia que se fue
por la que ya no sé llorar

deseo renunciar a ese privilegio

jaguar´s roar
   *Raquel Martínez-Gómez, Spain*
   *Translated by*
   *Ana García-Casillas Martínez-Gómez, Spain*

the inner voice roars
the poem's detail frightens me
with its promise of salvation

I know there's nothing like it
maybe just a fleeting moment of calm
the pleasure of beholding beauty

it opens and closes
and always comes to an end

I cling to quenching my thirst
     anyway
as the mad woman I am
grasping this instant that withers away
that I feel will stab me in the future

there's something no longer new...

the experience
   EXPERIENCE

added infinity when there was a first time
impossible to foresee the ending
it seemed the joy would last forever

the inner voice roars
and I know it does not cure bitterness
if anything  it recreates that search
that stumbles around like a blind woman
   ...afternoon is devoured by another dusk

128

maybe the voice is telling me something
using a scale to measure
the eternity of a stay now gone
for which I no longer know how to cry

I want to give up that privilege

## ŠUMSKA STAZA
*Šimo Ešić, Bosna i Hercegovina*

Na kraju njive, na rubu šume,
počinje – željno dočeka tu me.

Onda me vodi između stabala
kud su je stopala ljudska tabala.

Grane šumore, grlica guče,
ona me dublje u šumu vuče.

Gugut mi prija, šumor mi godi,
ona me vodi, vodi, i vodi...

Briše mi gradske iz oka slike –
jelike, jelike, samo jelike

i krošnje, krošnje, ogromne, nijeme –
kao da stižem u prošlo vrijeme.

Nestaje gradska vreva i cika,
cvrkut ptica, šumor jelika

i tihi život buba u travi
i mir od kog se vrti u glavi!

A ona ide, ide, vrluda,
preskoči potok, zaviri svuda,

penje se, slazi, a ja je pratim
i ne pomišljam da se vratim.

Ona se izvija, vijuga, mota
do kraja šume – ili života?!

Slušam tišinu, od sreće blistam –
možda ću i ja da prolistam!

# FOREST TRAIL
*Šimo Ešić, Bosnia*
*Translated by Aleksandra Radulović, Serbian*


At the end of the field, the edge of the forest,
It begins – and welcomes me eagerly honest.

Then leads me between the trees
where the people walk with ease.

Branches rustle, a turtle dove coos,
it drags me deeper into the woods.

I like the coo, the rustle is pleasing,
it leads me, leads me, and leads me ...

Deletes the city images from my eyes -
Firs, firs, and nothing but firs that rise

And treetops, those crowns, silent and huge-
as if I travel to long lost refuge

The hustle and bustle of the city in my ears,
is blurred by the chirping, the rustling of firs

and the quiet life of beetles in the grass
and the peace that makes your worries pass

And it goes, leads, wanders around,
skips the creek, peeks inside and out

it climbs, descends, I follow the track

without even thinking of going back.
It twists and bends like nothing else
to the end of the forest - or life itself?!

I listen to the silence, I'm happy to tell
maybe I will be blossoming as well!

# THE BLOSSOM FORECAST
### *Simon Fletcher, England*


From February, blackthorn will turn the hedgerows
white, across the shires.

Late March, heavy snowfalls of wild cherry flowers
will spread north up the river Severn.

In April expect storms of pink and white apple blow
in the west, especially around Hereford,

a hail of creamy pear blossom in the Teme valley
from Worcester up to Ludlow.

Japanese-delicate plum flowers will sprinkle
the Vale of Evesham.

And, finally, expect squalls of damson petals,
just about anywhere.

# SONG THRUSH, DOLGOCH
### *Simon Fletcher, England*

The song thrush perches on the ash,
above the broken quarry rocks,
and sings a medley, tuneful, loud;
to chilly ears such joy he brings.

A ballad, pop, a waltz then jazz,
a thumping hymn and choral line;
it teaches all of music's modes,
rung out by chance, and mixed by whim.

The thrush displays to catch the ear,
this polyphonic friend of March,
with speckled notes in many moods,
and brighter than the greenest larch.

## ANTWORT EINER BLINDEN
*Susanna Piontek, USA/Deutschland*

"Was ist für dich Frühling?"
frage ich die blinde alte Frau.
Sie seufzt und lächelt.
"Frühling ist lebendig,
ist voller Vogelstimmen,
die mich schon in der Frühe
mit schönen Liedern wecken.
Frühling duftet nach Natur.
Ich sehe das Grün nicht,
aber vermeine, es zu riechen.
Wenn der Wind den Geruch
frischgemähten Grases zu
mir aus Nachbars Garten trägt,
bin ich glücklich.
Stundenlang können meine Finger
die kleinen Weidekätzchen liebkosen,
zarte Pelzkugeln, mit denen man sich
sanft über die Wange streichen kann.
Frühlingsregen ist anders als in
den übrigen Jahreszeiten, und
Frühlingswind hält immer
Überraschungen bereit.
Steht er noch mit einem Fuß
im Winter und ist eisig kalt?
Oder ist es bereits warm geworden
und er erfrischt?
Vielleicht lehnt er sich schon
Richtung Sommer und gleicht
der Luft aus einem warmen Fön?

Frühling ist Beginn und Verheißung,
er ist Abschütteln von Altem.
Der Kreislauf beginnt von Neuem.
Für mich ist Frühling die
schönste Zeit im Jahr,
eine Zeit der Dankbarkeit.
Der Winter ist vorbei.
Und ich bin noch da."

# RESPONSE OF A BLIND WOMAN
### *Susanna Piontek, USA/Germany*

"What is spring to you?"
I ask the blind old woman.
She sighs and smiles.
"Spring is alive,
is full of bird songs,
that wake me up early in the morning
with beautiful melodies.
Spring smells of nature.
I can't see the green,
but I think I can smell it.
When the wind brings the scent
of freshly mown grass to me
from the neighbor's garden,
I am happy.
For hours my fingers can caress
the little pussy willows,
delicate balls of fur, with which
one can gently stroke
one's cheek.
Spring rain is different than
in the other seasons, and
spring wind always has
surprises in store.
Does it still have one foot
in winter and is it freezing cold?
Or has it already become warm
and refreshing?
Maybe it already leans
toward summer and resembles
the warm air from a hair dryer?

Spring is the beginning and promise,
it is shaking off the old.
The cycle begins anew.
For me spring is the
most beautiful time of the year,
a time of gratitude.
Winter is over.
And I'm still here."

## DIE FAHNEN, DIE STÖRCHE
*Utz Rachowski, Deutschland*


*„Im Vorfeld dieses Krieges haben die Polen*
*ihre historische Chance verpasst,*
*das Maul zu halten."*
(Der französische Staatspräsident im März 2003)

Dieser Frühling
der lügt
malte meine Tage
schwarz
in den Kalender

In diesem Frühling
der so täuschte
sind die Störche
angekommen
in Europa wieder
nur die nach Polen
flogen
blieben aus

Die polnischen du weißt
die Vögel
das kennst du ja von mir
nehmen
einen andern
ihren eignen Weg
anders als alle
ziehen über Euphrat Tigris

In diesem Frühling
der so trog
und es war Krieg
blieben aus die Störche
die nach Polen wollten
das kennst du ja
sind erschossen
gestorben wer weiß
kehrten um in der Welt
wohin
das kennst du ja
von mir

Ob den Polen nun
die Farben fehlen
für ihre Fahnen
Rot und Weiß
wer weiß es schon
aber das Schwarz

wohin
dein schönstes Schwarz
Dass ich noch sterben
Muss
all dies der Tod
mein Gott
das hatt ich völlig
jetzt vergessen
durch dich
nun ganz und gar
seit jenem Tag
als ich dich
wiedersah

In diesem Frühling
unsrem
in dem du mich verrietst
du weißt wofür
du weißt an wen
so zeitig
blieb ich aus
und halte
jetzt mein Maul

Fehlt deinem Mund
die Farbe nun
den Wangen etwas noch
du lachst schon wieder
und hisstest deine Fahne neu
Ich nahm nur Schwarz mit
von den Farben
dein schönes Schwarz
von dir
das kennst du ja an mir
anders als alle
riss ich dir ab
die Totenmaske

Und der Frühling
der so fälschte
malte schwärzer
meine Tage
in den Kalender
deinen bunten

142

# FLAGS AND STORKS
*Utz Rachowski, Germany*
*Translated by Louise E. Stoehr, USA*

> *"In the run-up to this war, the Poles*
> *missed their historic opportunity*
> *to keep their mouths shut."*
> (The French President in March, 2003)

This spring
that tell lies
painted my days
black
in the calendar

During this spring
that so deceived
the storks
arrived
again in Europe
only those who flew
to Poland
stayed away

You see, the Polish
birds
you know that from me
take
a different path
their own
different from all others
and migrate over Euphrates and Tigris

This spring
that was so deceptive
and there was war
so the storks heading
to Poland stayed away
you know that
were shot
died turned around
in the world who knows
to where
you know that
from me

If for the Poles now
are lacking the colors
for their flags
red and white
who even knows
and yet the black

to where
your most beautiful black
That I still must
die
all this, death
my God
I'd completely
forgotten that just now
on your account
now entirely
since that day
when I again
saw you

During this spring
ours
when you betrayed me
you know what for
you know to whom
so early
I stayed away
and now keep
my mouth shut


While your mouth now
is lacking in color
as are your cheeks a bit
you're laughing again
and raised your flag anew
I took only black with me
of the colors
your beautiful black
from you
you know that about me
different from all others
tore it off you
your death mask

And the spring
that so deluded
painted even blacker
my days
in the calendar
your colorful calendar

# SO AM ERSTEN WARMEN TAG
*Uwe Friesel, Deutschland*

So am ersten warmen Tag
wenn einem der Wind
so durch das Hemd weht  die Sonne
so auf den Bauch
      im Gesträuch
und Dampfer tuten ab und zu
      auf der Elbe
und du liegst da und
keiner redet dazwischen
      und die Sonne
      und Ameisen
      und der nächste Schornstein
einen Kilometer weg

# ABOUT THE FIRST WARM DAY
*Uwe Friesel, Germany*


About the first warm day
when a breeze
leaks through your t-shirt  and sun
on your tummy
            'tween the bushes
and now and then a steamer hoots
            from Elbe river below
and you're lying there and
nobody disturbs us
            and the sun
            and ants
            and the next chimney
a mile away

# CEA MAI ÎNALTĂ DECORAȚIE A LUMII
*Valentin Iacob, România*


La început, plutește însingurată peste ierburi și printre
copaci,
O apariție cu pielea de abur
și muguri de stele,

Atât de frumoasă și uneori așa prețioasă
încât prin livezi, mugurii întâi ei îi cer voie
să se spargă.
După care o pun să le aleagă
Și culoarea petalelor ...

Dar cel mai greu a fost când într-un an ea și-a dorit,
și bătea din picior,
un cais negru
cu florile negre și
caisele negre
și-un canar negru
cu ciocul verde,
cocoțat în cais.

Un canar arțăgos
scormonind îndârjit din aripi
și noroc,

Canarul care cântă primăvara, iar și iar,
victorioasă printre aburii visului;

Primăvara cu mantia ei din muguri de stele
– și-o panglică albastră –

cea mai înaltă decorație
pe care-o primim toți, an de an  ...

# THE HIGHEST HONOR IN THE WORLD
*Valentin Iacob, Romania*
*Translated by George Volceanov, Romania*

Wrapped in loneliness,
It first hovers above the grass and the trees,
A misty-skinned apparition with starry buds,

So beautiful and so precious at times,
That when it floats through the orchards,
The buds ask for her permission before
Bursting forth.
Then, they ask her to pick out the color of their petals
...

But the hardest was the year when
She threw a tantrum as
She badly wanted a black apricot-tree
With black blossoms,
And black apricots,
And a black green-beaked canary,
Perched upon a branch in the apricot-tree.

A grouchy canary,
Violently flapping its wings and its luck,
A canary, chirping, again and again,
Praising the glory of spring through the mist of a
dream;

Spring with its mantle woven from starry buds
– And a blue ribbon –

The highest honor granted
To each of us every year ...

# કૂંડામાં મારો ચંપો

વર્ષા દાસ, ભારત

કૂંડામાં તે કંઈ ચંપો ઊગે ?
એ તો વૃક્ષ છે.
ભલે ને કૂંડું મોટું અને મજબૂત હોય !
કૂંડામાં ચંપો જોઈને એક મિત્રે ટકોર કરી ,
'આ તે કેવું બોન્ઝાઇ ! નાનુંયે નહિ અને મોટુંયે નહિ !'

વૃક્ષ ભલે કૂંડામાં , તોયે ચારેય ઋતુઓ માણે .
કપરા શિયાળામાં બધાં પણ તજે
ડાળીઓ દેખાય ઠૂંઠી, નાગી ને બોડી ,
પણ મૂળિયાં મજબૂત કરે.

દિવસો તો સૌના બદલાય
ચંપા, ચમેલી ને ગુલાબના પણ.
શિયાળાનું પ્રસ્થાન થયું ને વસંતનું આગમન.
એનો પગરવ ન સંભળાય, પણ ચંપાનો હરખ ન માય.
એની ડાળે ટશિયા ફૂટ્યા, ને પાંદડાં હળવેથી ઊગ્યાં,
ટોચ પાર અને ડાળોની વચ્ચોવચ પણ.

વસંતને વધાવતાં આ પાંદડાં માણસ કરતાંયે વધુ સંવેદક.
હવા, પ્રકાશને હોંકારો દે, સુષુપ્ત પ્રાણને પ્રગટાવે !
વસંતને આલિંગતો આ કૂંડાનો ચંપો
ફૂલો વરસાવીને પ્રેમથી વધાવે !
મારી કહાણીયે કૂંડાના ચંપા સમી.
કડકડતી ટાઢમાં મજબૂત થઇ, ને પછી...ફૂટી પડ્યા અનેક રંગ,
કદાચ આ જ છે મારી વસંત !

# MY POTTED CHAMPA TREE
*Varsha Das, India*

How can a Champa tree grow in a pot?
It's a tree after all,
Even if the pot is big and strong!
Noticing my Champa, a friend quipped,
'What kind of Bonsai is this? It's neither small, nor big!"

Even in the pot it enjoys all seasons.
Sheds its leaves in harsh winter,
looks a little ugly, bald and nude,
 but continues to strengthen its roots.

The time doesn't stop for any one of us,
It's the same for the Champa, Jasmine or Rose.
Winter has left, Spring has walked in.
I couldn't hear her steps, but Champa knew it well.
A burst of Spring was seen in the branches,
leaves began to sprout on each branch of the tree.

Welcoming the Spring, with the heart warmer than man
 tree's outbreak of energy, reached out for light and air.
Showering white flowers, my potted Champa tree
with all its love, embraced the Spring!

The story of the potted tree is similar to mine.
I grew stronger in frigid winter, and then... a burst of colors,
perhaps that was my Spring!

# A SPRING DAY
*William S. Peters, Sr., USA*

Sister and Brother,
6 & 8
Sitting by the window,
Looking out
At yet another
Beautiful Spring day

The weather was inviting,
The sun was shining,
Yet,
They were forlorned,
For what is the use
Of going outside
To play,
If you can not play
With your friends

They tired of the activities
That Mommy had invented
In the attempts
To distract them,
And TV was boring

They had mastered all the video games,
So they relegated themselves
Once again
To playing with
Imaginary characters
Just like they used to do

On rainy days . . .
But now,
It is Spring
Ad many things
Have come,
Blossomed and buzzed
To distract them
From their mundane

Their wonder has been stimulated,
Heightened,
And there is no turning back.

This is just another
Spring Day

# LET US BE SPRING FILLED
*William S. Peters, Sr., USA*

i tire of Death
and the regenerative energies
that life affords us
in this season
winter

i do understand it's purpose
and it is necessary
i think

i am feeling full of expectation
i am living this day
in the Spring
i am growing
in a knowing
that i can continue sowing
seeds of hope
regardless the time of year

i will dig a hole
in the frozen soils of my consciousness
and plant seeds
anyway

i will nurture them
with the warmth of my love
and pour my re-intensified spirit
upon them

they WILL sprout, bud and leaf
and blossom
and the fruit will be early
and sweet
for i have changed my own seasons
unto my pleasing
and the limits
no longer exist
upon the equator
of my understanding

let us be Spring filled

# 春季发布：泽费罗斯vs.芙洛拉

/中国/殷晓媛

"拒绝阿波罗的达芙妮化为月桂树，拒绝河神的阿瑞梭莎遁形为叙拉古的泉水……是否在父权体系神话框架中，拒绝的自由与不情愿的毁灭被捆绑售卖？
我，芙洛拉，指着绝地复生的万物，指着晨昏激荡的日月，发誓捍卫自己说'不'的权利！"

"快些换上昭告天下的新娘装吧，这天地间茫茫大荒是我泽费罗斯的秀场。"

那催发紊流的傲慢身形伫立在母亲厄俄斯祷祝过的海岸，挥动羊鞭将潮头白浪从晨曦的樱桃红前调中分离，沙滩上横亘一道
茶色玫瑰口红痕。若此时他张开双臂向后仰去，从洒金桃红浅滩中拔地而出的兄弟们
将飞升并临空接住他缠裹血色丝绦的冰冷肘腕：东风之神欧洛斯贴缀蝶形茛绸眼影，拖曳海洋云母光在身后晃漾
南风之神诺特斯赤裸胸膛心形领枫叶披肩垂下日光流苏，北风之神博瑞阿斯冰魅东蓝鸲唇妆，后背翅根长出铜绿鹿角树枝
泽费罗斯指挥他们与虞美人花田一同澎湃起伏。"作为一种暴怒的能量，风的角度与力度有时都会失控，我在此向沉睡的海辛瑟斯致以悲悼。"

"这算是威胁吗？"芙洛拉头顶绿桔梗+绿玫瑰+大花蕙兰冠饰、身着框架庞大繁花锦袍走出画面时，几乎带倒与裙边蓝色花朵长久以来长成一体的背景墙

她穿行的镂空刻纸空间雪纺蕾丝玉兰香草真假难辨。拱门下令箭荷花喷吐琼白细蕊，踢脚线边使君子随水彩画笔抛伸线条

花毛茛随她说话音量膨圆，沙巴茉莉在她长拖尾上堆满隆冬剩余的雪

檀香雪松琥珀桃金娘香氛沿途织出浮雕感沙画。此时即使卖花姑娘顶着麻纱与烂花绒剪裁头花与满头纷披的缎带走出，也难免得到风雾的厚待

"世间众花的钥匙握在我手。驱遣西风来索要吧，留给你的只有旷野与沉船。"


超模1：
花束开放延时摄影视频LED背投。玫瑰、曼陀罗、虎皮百合、鹤望兰、水仙、山桃花、曼珠沙华、鸢尾、大丽花和茶花蒙太奇剪辑。模特面孔顺睡莲绽开方向螺旋形打光

锁骨上蓝色满天星标本状粘贴。孔雀羽毛在敞领处形成漩涡。模特从凋敝松石蓝船舱中站起，背景中花朵便在苏打气泡中化为石头

超模2：
"帝王血"郁金香造型单肩礼服。藕臂上段有白羽及云彩纹身。她蒙着眼，从架设半空的跳板上姗姗走过

天堑彼岸花树站成逆光中的烛台。模特回眸，打响指，一朵向日葵怒放，再一打响指，木芙蓉绽开

烈日下她撕扯掉胸口巨大荷叶边花瓣，隐藏的繁花芍药状膨胀，迅速炸满了屏幕……

据奥维德《岁时记》记载，并经波提切利《春》印证，我以武力绑架了你，将你变成我的妻子，你才从克洛丽丝成为了芙洛拉。你怎么能擅自篡改剧本？"
"你什么时候才能明白，芙洛拉并不需要谁改造她、册封她、支配她。盛开是造物赋予的权力，西风能做的不过是为我欢呼而已。"

西风之神不甘地追逐着芙洛拉，穿过山坡、湖泊和高原，所至之处染为鹅黄嫩绿。她并不惊慌逃跑。她转身在他们之间投掷下一串种子——它们噼里啪啦长成向夕阳倾斜的参天花墙

## SPRING 2021 RUNWAY SHOW:
## ZEPHYRUS VS. FLORA

*YIN Xiaoyuan, China*

"Daphne was transformed into a laurel tree, and
Arethusa was turned into a fountain in Syracuse...
Each frame of scene in the history of patriarchal
system is about abuse and coercion: to lead a life
against your will or to die for freedom...
I, Flora, swear by everything restored to life at the
turning of seasons, by the eternal sun and ever-
changing moon, that I will spare no effort to defend
my legal right to say 'NO'!"

"Put on your bridal dress so I can start to make the
wedding announcement. You should know that the
endless stretch of wilderness under the sky is MY
runway!"

The arrogant stalwart figure was standing on the
shore, which his mother Eos had blessed with her
divine morning glow. Zephyrus drove the snow-white
tides ashore with his whip, so it parted naturally with
the rosy head notes of morn lingering on the horizon.
There appeared a mysterious stroke of Tangerine
lipstick on the beach
If at this moment he fell backwards freely with his
arms stretched out, his brothers standing waist-deep
in the mahogany-color shallows would rose above
water and catch him from underneath
by the elbows and wrists, which were pale and cold
and wrapped with scarlet ribbons: Eurus was wearing
gambier-silk ornaments around his eyes, which
reflected the pearly glimmers over the ocean behind
him

Notus, bare-chested, had his cloak draped around him, there were golden tassels hanging from its heart shaped neckline; Boreas' lips were as cold as ice and as blue as eastern-bluebird feathers, brighter than his verdigris-covered antler-shaped wings
Zephyrus commanded them to roll with the corn poppy field. "As a form of rage, the wind can get out of hand at any moment, both in direction and velocity. My deepest condolences to those who think they lost Hyacinthus!"

"Is that a threat?" Flora showed herself with a headdress decorated with green Eustoma+green roses+green boat orchids. When she walked forward in her Rococo dress with its immense bustle cage, covered by big fluorescent flowers, she nearly brought down the dramatic backdrop behind, whose bottom almost blended with the forget-me-not's on her long trail
She moved elegantly through the archway so the space full of chiffon flowers, white laces, vanilla and magnolia became a 3D paper craft mammoth.
Disocactus phyllanthoides flicked their immaculate tongues at the gates, and the Rangoon creeper climbed up walls like water color curves
Persian buttercups swelled out while she spoke aloud, and Arabian Jasmine heaped their virgin snow on her dress
Sandalwood, cedar, amber and myrtle fragrances weaved an atmosphere ahead like high-relief objects. What a paradise of hallucinations! Even a flower girl passing through here, with interlaced cambric and etched-out velvet flowers in her hair, would be embraced by popularity and prosperity once she went outside

160

"All flowers in the world are under my command. I hold the key. Come, defeat me and take it! Or admit that you have lost and back down to your wreck!"

Supermodel A:
Ground supported LED screen. Time-lapse photography of roses, Datura flowers, tiger lilies, crane flowers, daffodils, peach blossoms, red spider lilies, irises, dahlias and camellias. Supermodel's face was right beneath the water lily which opened its petals clockwise
There were twigs of blue baby's breath on her collarbones, and peacock feathers interlocked above her breasts. Supermodel rose from the bench in the cabin, and everything turned into stone behind her in the wreck

Supermodel B:
She was in a red one-shoulder dress designed in the shape of a Kingsblood tulip. She had doves&clouds tattoos on her upper arms. Being blind-folded, she walked calmly upon the gangplank
A big lone tree beyond the rift valley suddenly turned dim and vague, like a multi-branched candelabrum. Supermodel looked back at it over her shoulder and snapped her fingers, a sunflower came into bloom under the tree, she snapped again and a cotton rose mallow was lit up in pink luster there
In the blazing sun she tore open a "lotus-petal" from the front of her dress, and hidden peony buds burst out from under her neckline and crowded over the camera...

"According to 'The Fasti' by Ovid, which scene was also endorsed by 'Primavera' by Sandro Botticelli, I am supposed to rape/kidnap you and make you,

Chloris, into Flora. How dare you tamper with the original scripts?"
"When can you realize that Flora never needed anyone to convert her, give her a title and make her obey. I am FULL BLOOM. I am PRIME. Your west wind can contribute nothing to Spring but applauses."

Zephyrus chased Flora up the hills, over the lakes and across the highlands, squandering a profusion of green color everywhere. Flora did not run but walked on at a sedate pace, turning around and threw a handful of seeds before him...and boom! The seeds grew into a boundless floral wall leaning towards the sunset

# SPRINGTIME HAS ARRIVED
*Simone Seym, USA*


it's time for change
and that time is now
nature is greening
temperatures are rising
so much is blooming
what a wonderful day

it's time for change
philonise in solidarity
with the wrights
united in grief
do you remember
the fragrance of love

it's time for change
no knees on necks
no accidental shots
daunted called his mom
we are with you miss katie
miss wright heard his last

when will this come to an end
springtime has arrived ...

# Η ΧΡΗΣΙΜΟΤΗΤΑ ΤΗΣ ΟΜΟΡΦΙΑΣ
## *Γιώργος Χουλιάρας Ελλάδα*

Είναι τόσο όμορφα χρήσιμη αυτή η κούπα
που υγρό χωρίς να φεύγει από τα χέρια μου
κρατά συνεχώς το πρώτο ρόφημα της ημέρας
ώστε καθώς αρχίζει πάλι να αναδεύεται
η σκέψη μέσα στην κούπα του μυαλού
δεν μπορώ παρά να συμπεράνω ότι τίποτε
δεν είναι χρησιμότερο από την ομορφιά
όπως εσύ κάθε πρωί άλλωστε μου θυμίζεις
αν και ακόμη θα κοιμάσαι κάπου μακριά

# THE USEFULNESS OF BEAUTY
*Yiorgos Chouliaras, Greece*
*Translated by David Mason,*
*USA/Tasmani and the author*



It is so beautifully useful this cup
that keeps the liquid from escaping my hands
and holds unbrokenly the first drink of the day
so when thought again begins to stir
in the cup of the mind
I can only surmise that nothing
is more useful than beauty
as after all you remind me every morning
though you are still sleeping far away

# ABRIL
*Yuray Tolentino Hevia, Cuba*

con la primavera/ viene una ansiedad/
de pájaro preso/ que quiere volar.
José Martí

Abril esconde bajo sus raíces
el polvo de las quimeras
y las flores destinadas a enamorar
en las avenidas.

Un susurro de esperanza
late en los bulbos
mientras los amigos
cuelgan en las ventanas
los abrazos que huelen a limón.

Nace de la tierra la lluvia de otoño
en follaje y vuelo de mariposa
en el verso infinito
que guarda la luz de la aurora
y la soledad del cuadro
al apagar la luz.

Nadie sabe porque en abril los poetas
lloran pétalos al decir la tarde adiós.
Está naciendo la primavera
desnuda, sin que venga las cigüeñas
agitada y rebelde
como la voz del arroyo
en la garganta de la roca.

# APRIL
*Yuray Tolentino Hevia, Cuba*
*Translated by Leidy Díaz Hevia, Cuba*

with spring/comes an anxiety /
of a prisoner bird/that wants to fly.
Jose Martí

April hides under its roots
the dust of chimeras
and the flowers destined to fall in love
on the avenues.

A whisper of hope
beats in the bulbs
while friends
hang in the windows
the hugs that smell like lemon.

The autumn rain is born from the earth
in foliage and butterfly flight
in the infinite verse
that guards the light of dawn
and the loneliness of the painting
when turning off the light.

Nobody knows why poets in April
petals cry as the afternoon say goodbye.
Spring is being born
naked, without the storks coming
restless and rebellious
like the voice of the stream
in the gorge of the rock.

# IST FRÜHLING ZEITGERECHT?
*Zorin Diaconescu, Rumänien*

Die einsame Rose wäre bei Christian Morgenstern
auffindbar
selbst wenn deren rote Farbe Unpässlichkeiten
verursacht
ist das Zufall oder Sonderfall?...
einfacher ist es mit dem blauen Band
das uns Herr Mörike hinterließ,
rein farblich wäre letzteres weniger engagiert,
ist eher vertrauenserweckend...

Weil wir über den Frühling der Dichter reden
wobei wir uns keinen eigenen Frühling leisten
das konnte seiner Zeit noch Joseph Freiherr von
Eichendorff -

Wir sind abhängig von globalen Wetterverhältnissen
dabei hängt Zustimmung vom Netz ab

Wir haben noch keine Frühlingspartei
und bieten dementsprechend den Wählern bloß
unsere Erinnerungen und wer soll sie verstehen?
Erinnerungen sind logisch generationsbedingt
und leider gibt es keinen Frühling 2.0

# IS SPRING STILL IN?
*Zorin Diaconescu, Romania*

The red rose could be found with Christian
Morgenstern
even if its color causes ailments
this might be a coincidence or a special case
it is easier with the blue ribbon
that Mr. Mörike left us
purely in terms of color, the latter would be less
committed
and is rather trustworthy

Because we're talking about the poets' spring
while we cannot afford our own spring
Baron Joseph von Eichendorff was able to do that in
his day -

We are dependent on global weather conditions
consent depends on the network

We don't have a spring party yet
and accordingly no bids for the voters
but our memories and who should understand them?
Memories are logically generational
and unfortunately there is no spring 2.0

# SPRING : A WILD BEAST
*Yuyutsu Sharma, Nepal/India*

> *Spring unfurls its blue ribbon*
> Eduard Mörike

The cracked patch
of a clammy honeycomb comes

dripping out of a sobbing night
and clings to the frozen calf of my leg.

There's a scent of spring
back again to dance in my nostrils,

its pungent air
suffused with a stinging odor

of a bonfire
of sandalwood, butter, sesame,

cinnamon and honey
aflame somewhere across

the icy rivers
of our shrunken canyons.

I leap out of the bed
and thump my foot to let it

fall off to the grassy ground,
homeless bees buzzing in slow motion

in the stabbing sunlight
of a wounded day in our  boorish republic.

Don't panic, just keep quiet,
I whisper, seeing she's about to scream.

They  mustn't sense our fears,
the fright to live in a plague is to suffer

the fate of a bonded sex-worker,
to endure the inevitable,

and in silence surrender to lethal
pleasure of the demented Deities.

Each moment a hazard,
each day a fresher revelation

of the master's disregard  of the corpses
piling up in newly-founded crematoriums.

I step out of the house
in the Himalayas to venture out

into our canyons aflame
from the flush of rhododendrons

tulips, primrose, cherry,
blue poppies, geraniums

and watch spring crouch
like a wild beast as it did a year ago

holding back the delight
to dance like a fat bumble bee

celebrating the arrival of
a succulent spring in our glistening valleys.

# BIOGRAPHIES

**Albrecht Classen** is University Distinguished Professor of German Studies at the University of Arizona. He has currently published 115 scholarly books and close to 800 articles. But he is also an active poet with nine volumes of his own poems under his belt, and four volumes of satires and essays. He is the current President of the Society of Contemporary American Literature in German (SCALG), and a regular contributor to the literary journal Trans-Lit2.

**Ali Al-Hazmi** Born in (Damad) – Saudi Arabia (1970). Participated in numerous recitals of poetry inside and outside of Saudi Arabia: International Poetry Festival Costa Rica 2013-Toledo, Spain 2014-Punta del Este, Uruguay  2015-Madrid. Spain 2016-Havana, Cuba 2016- Medellín, Colombia 2016-Istanbul-Turkey, 2016- Roma 2017-Romania 2017. The world Grand prize (for Poetry ) International Academy Orient-Occident in Romania 2017. Medal of honor to the poetic and literary merit in the XIV  Encuentro Internacional Poetas y Narradores De las Dos Orillas y 4o Congreso de Literatura 2015, Punta del Este Uruguay. The poem (A street through a wall). Arab and international critics wrote about his poetic production. Has eight printed books translated to different languages.

**Anna Würth** is an author and photographic artist. Her poems and short stories have been published in 83 anthologies and by Wachholtz in her book „Aphrodite.Lovestoned". In 2001 she received the Literary Sponsorship Award of GEDOK. In her 'Literary Pictures' she combines her poems with her photography. They were exhibited in Hamburg, Denmark and Cyprus.
Dr John Waterfield (translator), Doctorate in English literature in Oxford. Translator for 25 years.


**Annabel Villar** – Poet and cultural activist. Founding member Liceo Poetico de Benidorm; Associate Academic and Honorary Member American Academy of Modern Literature; Director "Azul" Poetry Collection and International Poetry Festival "Benidorm & Costa Blanca"; Founding Member Student Academy of Contemporary Art (Rio de Janeiro, Brazil, Chair No. 6 "Gabriela Mistral").


**Antje Stehn**, born in Germany, resides in Italy. She is a poet, visual artist, video producer, art curator. She is curating the international art-poetry project "Rucksack a Global Poetry Patchwork" since 2020. She is part of the international collective "Poetry is my Passion" which organizes transcultural events in Milan. She is editing the international poetry voice "Milano, una città mille lingue" for the poetry magazine TamTamBumBum and is co-editor in the Latin-American Blog Los Ablucionistas and the Blog Teerandaz in Bangladesh. She is member of the scientific committee of the Piccolo Museo della Poesia of Piacenza, Italy.

Her poems are translated into Italian, English, Polish, Macedonian, and Spanish.


***Aristea Papalexandrou*** was born in Hamburg in 1970. She has published six books of poetry: She has studied music and Medieval and Modern Greek Literature. She works as an editor. For her last book, It's Passing Us By, she had honored by the Academy of Athens, in December 2017.
Translator: Philip Ramp, born in Michigan, is a poet and experienced translator who has been living and working in Greece for over thirty five years. He has published numerous volumes of original poetry, and done many translations from the Greek.


***Ayça Erdura*** wrote 20 pieces of lyrics for her famous singer father Ersan Erdura. While she was conducting the poetry exhibition called "Journey Of Poetry" organized in 2018, she herself participated in this exhibition with her 13 visual poems. She acts as the Project coordinator and master of ceremony for Seyhan Livaneli Short Story Contest. Her poems appeared in literary magazines. Her book called "Zarf Zihin-Envolope Mind" got special attention for her creative interpretation she applied in the book format at "Poetry Horse Seyhan Erözçelik First Book Poetry Prize Contest".

Translator Tozan Alkan is a lecturer at Istanbul University, Department of Foreign Languages. PEN Writers Association, Writers Union of Turkey, the Association of Authors and ÇEVBİR members.


174

**Betty Gilmore** poet and blues singer, born in Oklahoma, raised in Los Angeles, Studies in Latin American culture at UCLA. Volunteer work as a teacher in Costa Rica. Studied poetry at the L.A Woman's Building Feminist Studio Workshop. Begins to combine poetry and blues to raise awareness of African-American culture, extending her interest to include other world cultures. In Milan, she dedicates herself to transcultural activities, cultural interaction and anti-racism. Has published  numerous articles, poems and music. Belongs to the international poetry collective, Poetry is My Passion sponsored by the Cubearte Association .

**Burkhard P. Bierschenck**, born 1950, spent a part of his youth in the Middle and the Far East. He studied journalism, history and literature (Master) and visited the famous German Journalist's School in Munich. He speaks and writes in German, English and French. Apart from his career as Journalist, reaching top positions of Editorial Director and General Manager, he wrote more than 25 books, mostly novels and poetry. His acclaimed poetry became part of school curriculum. He was honored with memberships of PEN Club, HOMER (Historical writers association), SYNDIKAT (Crime writers Association), UNION DES POÈTES (French Poets Association).

**Chloe Koutsoubelli.** Her first collection of poems was published when she was twenty-two years old and she continues to write and publish ever since for thirty six years now. She has written ten collections of poetry, two novels and two theatrical plays. Her work has been translated in German, French, Spanish,

Bulgarian, Italian, Turkish and English. She has participated with her poems in many Greek and foreign language Anthologies. Many of her poems and short stories have been published in Greek and foreign language magazines. Her collection of poems with the title "Those who eat in the same table in another land" won the National award of Poetry of 2016.

**Christine Geweke** is a painter, sculptor and poetess. She is a former board member of the Hamburg Authors' Association and heads the art room for lyric, paintings and sculptures. On 8.3.2009 she launched the *Charta der SchriftstellerInnen für die Wahrung des Weltfriedens* (charta of authors for the keeping of the world peace) und starts publishing anthologies with peaceful notions. Has published about seven volumes of poetry:
Translator: Benjamin Geweke, student


**Christopher Okemwa** is a literature lecturer at Kisii University, Kenya. He has a PhD in performance poetry from Moi University, Kenya. He is the founder and current director of Kistrech International Poetry festival in Kenya (www.kistrechpoetry.org). His novella, Sabina and the Mystery of the Ogre, won the Canadian Burt Award for African Literature in 2015. He has written eight books of poetry and been translated to Armenian, Chinese, Greek, Norwegian, Finnish, Hungarian, Arabic, Polish, Chinese, Nepalese, Turkish, Russian, Spanish, Catalan and Serbian. He has also translated four literary works of international poets from English to Swahili.

176

He is the editor of Musings During a Time of Pandemic: A World Anthology of Poems on COVID-19 and I Can't Breathe: A Poetic Anthology of Social Justice, both of which feature over 550 international poets and are 1200-plus pages. He is the author of ten folktales of the Abagusii people of Kenya, three children's storybooks, one play, two novels and four oral literature textbooks.

***Claudia Piccinno***'s poems are in more than one hundred anthologies, she is a member of the jury in numerous national and international literary awards. She is the Director of the Word Festival for Poetry in Europe. She is board director for Galaktika Atunis Magazine and editor for Europe in the international magazine Papirus. She has received more than 200 awards in important national and international poetry competitions. She writes for a lot of international literary newspapers, blogs, e-magazine. She has published many poetry books and some essays in Italian and English, her works have been translated in French, Serbian, German, Turkish, Arabic, Chinese, Swedish and polish languages.

***Daniel Calabrese*** is an Argentinian poet born in Dolores city, Buenos Aires province. Lives in Santiago de Chile, where he became involved with the poetry and literary life of his adopted nation. Among his books of poetry, one must mention such titles as La faz errante, which won the Alfonsina Prize, and Oxidario, Prize from the National Arts Fund in Buenos Aires, as well as his book Ruta Dos, winner of the Prize Revista de Libros in Chile. His poetic work has received the approval of specialized critics in several

countries. Translated partially to Italian, English, French, Chinese and Japanese. Founder and director of Ærea, an annual magazine of poetry and translation.
Translator Katherine Hedeen has been a professor at Kenyon College (Ohio, USA). Her research interests include literary translation and Spanish-Caribbean literatures and cultures. She is a specialist in Latin American poetry, and translated many respected authors.

***Deborah D'Agostino***. Poet, writer, cultural events creator, Knight of Merit-Italy. BPW Italy member, lives in Rome, where for the past twenty five years she has been an organizer and presenter of cultural events. Has published poetry collections, translated also in English, French, German, Turkish and Arab, and religious poems in many publications. Winner of numerous national and international prizes for her poetry published in anthologies, magazines and art catalogues.Translator Helen Guyatt, Oxford, UK


***Don Krieger*** is a biomedical researcher whose focus is the electric activity within the brain. He is author of the 2020 hybrid collection, "Discovery" (Cyberwit), the 2022 hybrid chapbook, "When Danger Is Past, Who Remembers" (Milk and Cake Press), a 2020 Pushcart nominee, and  a 2020 Creative Nonfiction Foundation Science-as-Story Fellow. His work has appeared in American Journal of Nursing, Neurology, Seneca Review, The Asahi Shimbun, The Blue Nib, The Pittsburgh Post-Gazette,  and others, and has been translated into Farsi, Greek, Italian, German, and Turkish.

**Dorel Cosma**, Romania, holds a B.A. in Journalism, radio-tv producer, senior editor of several newspapers and magazines, chairman of the I.G.F. World Folklore Union, former manager of the Palace of Culture, the most important cultural institution of his hometown. Author of several books published in Romania, Bulgaria, Italy, Greece, Egypt, France, Argentina, Germany, Austria, Spain and the U.S.A.


**Elçin Sevgi Suçin** is a poet from Turkey. Her poems and essays on poetry appeared in various literary magazines. She published two poetry collections in Turkish. Her third poetry collection is currently under publication.

Neil P. Doherty is a translator born in Dublin, Ireland in 1972 who has resided in Istanbul since 1995. He currently teaches in Bilgi University. He is a freelance translator of both Turkish and Irish poetry.


**Emel Koşar** was born in Eskişehir (1981). In 2003, she graduated from Turkish Language and Literature Department of the Faculty of Arts and Sciences of Mimar Sinan University of Fine Arts. She is currently a faculty member at Turkish Language and Literature Department of Faculty of the Arts and Sciences of Mimar Sinan University of Fine Arts. She has published her poetry and essays on Turkish literature in various literary magazines. She published her research and review books, scientific and literary works she edited, and seven poetry collections.

Yasemin Kurtuluş was born in Istanbul in 1998. In 2016, she started her education in the Italian Language and Literature within Department of Western Languages and Literatures at Istanbul

University. She is currently continuing her education as a senior class in the same department.

**Emina Čabaravdić-Kamber**, born in Kakanj, Bosnia-Herzegovina, lived in Hamburg since 1968. She is a freelance writer, painter, and for 23 years teacher of exile literature and art in Hamburg, Lübeck, Münster, and Bosnia. She is a member of the German Writers' Union, of the German P.E.N. and the German Exile P.E.N. (German-speaking Authors Abroad) and the Foreign Press in Hamburg. In 1988 she founded the International Literary Club La Bohemina. She has received several literary awards and in 1996 was honored with the Medal of Merit of the Order of Merit of the Federal Republic of Germany for her literary work on peace and ending the war in Bosnia and Herzegovina.

**Erkut Tokman** is Turkish poet, actor, visual artist, editor and translator. He studied poetry, modern dance and acting in London, Bucharest and Milan. He is the member of Turkish and İtaly P.E.N-centers. He has published five poetry books. He won İtalian Ministry of Culture Translation Award -2019; "Messina Citta di Arta" and "Salvotore Quasimodo Jaci Poetry Awards.

Idil Karacadag is a freelance translator from Turkey. After acquiring her BA on Literature at Kadir Has University and spending a year at Bath Spa University, England as an exchange student, she is currently studying for an MA in English Literature at Bogazici University.

**George Wallace** is writer in residence at the Walt Whitman Birthplace, author of 38 chapbooks of poetry, and adjunct professor of English at Pace University in New York City. Heir to the American Beat and Whitman traditions, he performs his work worldwide, and has been translated into many European and South Asian languages. Winner of the Poetry Kit Best Book Award (UK), CW Post Poetry Prize (US), and festival laureateships in Albania, Macedonia, Bulgaria and Greece, he was named first laureate of the International Beat  Poetry Festival in 2018.

**Gino Leineweber** was born in 1944 and is working as a poet, writer, and translator since 1998. In between, he was editor of the German magazine Buddhistische Monatsblätter (BM) for six years. In terms of cultural policy, from 1991 to 2015, he was active as an elected deputy of the council of the Hamburg Authority of Culture. For twelve years, he led the Hamburg Authors' Association (HAV), and is currently a board member of the PEN Center German-Speaking Authors Abroad (formerly German Exile P.E.N). Having initially written and published novels and short stories, he is now publishing non-fiction and poetry. He writes in both German and American English. Since 2016, he has translated from English. His poetry has won numerous international awards.

**Gülname Albayrak**. Born in 1974 in Turkey, the artist studied painting at Uludağ University and then completed a master's degree in art at Istanbul Technical University. Pain, love, anxiety, fear,

desperation, nature, loneliness, rebellion, lack of communication are the subjects that she deal with in her poems. Includes metaphors in her poems. Aims to give people deep perspective.
Translator Ian Sinclair has been teaching students from all over the world. He is now retired and still enjoys his passion for painting.


**Hema Ravi,** freelance trainer for IELTS and Communicative English, is a poet, author, reviewer, independent researcher, event organizer and editor of Efflorescence (published by the Chennai Poets' Circle).  Her verses and write ups have been featured in several online and international print journals, noteworthy among them being the International Writers Journal (USA), Amaravati Poetic Prism (CCVA, Vijayawada), Culture and Quest ISISAR, Kolkata), and Setu, the Pittsburgh-based bilingual e-zine. She is among the 'Distinguished Writers 2021,' having secured the ninth place in the 9th Bharat Award for Literature International Short Story Contest.


**Hilal Karahan.** Turkish poetess, writer, translator, mother and medical doctor. She is born in 1977 in Gaziantep/Turkey. She has been writing professionally since 2000. She has joined many collective books, bilingual poetry almanacs and found in organization committee of international poetry festivals. She has six poetry, three prose books and many selected poem books published in different languages. She is recently a member of Turkey PEN, Intercontinental director of UNESCO linked World Festival of Poetry (WFP) organization, Turkey member of World Poetry Movement (WPM) and Turkish ambassador of World

Institute of Peace (WIP). She organizes the International FeminIstanbul Women's Poetry Festival every year since 2016. She has many national and international poetry awards. Since 2017, she is a member of the publishing council of international bilingual poetry magazines of Absent, Rosetta Word Literatura and Sahitya

**Holly Iglesias** has written three poetry collections – Sleeping Things, Angles of Approach, and Souvenirs of a Shrunken World – as well as a critical work, Boxing Inside the Box: Women's Prose Poetry. Her awards include fellowships from the National Endowment for the Arts, the North Carolina Arts Council, the Edward Albee Foundation, and the Massachusetts Cultural Council. Her current project is Theories of Flight, an intergenerational memoir in prose fragments.

**hülya n. yılmaz** [sic] is a published tri-lingual author, literary translator, and Director of Editing Services at Inner Child Press International, USA. Her poetic work has appeared in numerous anthologies of global endeavors and was presented at poetry events in the U.S. and abroad. In 2018, the WIN of British Colombia, Canada honored yılmaz with a literary excellence award. Her two poems remain permanently installed in Telepoem Booth. hülya [sic] finds it vital for everyone to understand a deeper sense of self, and writes creatively to attain a comprehensive awareness for and development of our humanity.

***Jenny Lkhagvasuren*** works as an English translator and Book Publisher in Mongolia. She started writing poems in 2013 and her first book of poetry "The Happy Lady" has been published both Mongolian and English. Some of her poems have been published in the Illinois State in USA, Turkey, Italy, Albany, Germany and India in poetry anthologies. She has translated several books from English to Mongolia and published in Mongolia, and aims to write prose besides poems and introduce Mongolian literature to the world.

***Juan C. Tajes***, Uruguay. Born 1946. Poet and multidisciplinary artist living in Holland since 1971. He writes poetry, theater, narrative and essay. Organizer of cultural events and give lectures on different subjects. His literary work is published and translated in different countries and participates in international literary festivals. Collaborates with literary magazines in the Netherlands, Argentina, Brazil, Turkey, Rumania, Germany and Mexico.

***Julio Pavanetti***. He is a poet, a cultural promoter, and the founder and President of the international poet's association "Liceo Poético de Benidorm" established in Spain. Director of the poetry collection "Azul" of Enkuadres Publishers, Alzira, Spain. Director of the International Poetry Festival "Benidorm & Costa Blanca" (FIPBECO). Member of the "Association of Spanish Writers and Artists". He has published thirteen books of poetry. He had received many awards, honors and recognitions, both for his poetry as for his cultural work. He has participated in several international summits and poetry festivals and

184

has been included in more than 80 international anthologies. Many of his poems have been translated into 26 different languages.

**Liana Sakelliou** is a Greek poet and professor in English at the Department of English Language and Literature, The University of Athens. For her academic and creative-writing activities she received two Fulbright awards, and grants from Princeton University, University of Coimbra, University of Sussex (West Dean), and The British Council. Her poems have appeared in numerous international anthologies, journals, and magazines, and have been translated into ten languages. Her 18 books with poems, scholarly articles, essays, and translations have been published in Greece, France, and the USA.

**Lily Exarchopoulou** is a novelist, poet, short story writer. She has studied, both in Greece and England, Ancient History and Archaeology as well as English and American Literature. She specializes in the 19th and 20th century novel. She has worked in educational institutes (University, High School) as well as a freelance translator, a journalist and a book reviewer. She has published three novels, two books of poetry (a third one will be published in 2021), 18 translations, one reader. Many of her short stories and poems have been published in anthologies, literary magazines, newspapers.

**Luz Stella Mejía** has published two books of poetry, Etimológicas (2020) and Palabras sumergidas (2018). Her writings have been included in anthologies and a short stories anthology. Her poem "That peace I want" won mention in "Thousand Poems for the Peace of the World, 2019". She lives in the US where she is editor in her publishing house Tessellata, and collects books in Spanish to share

**Mamta Sagar** is a noted Kannada poet, playwright and translator from India. Her writings focus on identity politics, feminism, issues around linguistic and cultural diversities. She has five poetry collections, four plays, poetry videos/films and many translations to her credit. Translations of her poems are published in several international literary journals. She is the founder of KAAVYA SANJE a community poetry engagement. Rucksack, an Art-Poetry installation project co-curated by Mamta Sagar with Antje Stehn is displayed at the Piccolo Museo della Poesia, Italy.

**Maren Schönfeld**, poetess and journalist. She has four poetry books and two non-fiction books published so far. In 2017 she received the Poetry Award from the Hamburg Authors' Association (Hamburger Autorenvereinigung).

**Marian Eikelhof** was born in Rotterdam, The Netherlands, in 1963. She is a poet who works in her daily life as a psychologist. Her work inspires her to write about the emotional aspects of life. Not only she describes in several languages about feelings of love, intimacy and desire, but also reflects about states of profound sadness and feelings of emptiness. On the whole she criticizes dehumanization and an on-going process of alienation in human relationships. Marian's poetry book "a zero hour contract with life" has been translated from Dutch into English and Turkish. Her poems have been published by several prestigious magazines and appear in a number of anthologies.

**Mesut Şenol** graduated from the Political Science Faculty of Ankara University. Earned his Master's Degree in Public Administration and Public Relations. His 11 poetry collections were published, and many of his poetry and literary translations appeared in many national and foreign literary publications and anthologies. A member of many literary organizations. He teaches at the Translation and Interpreting Studies Department of Yeditepe University, and also Communications at the Communications Department of Bahçeşehir University. He is the Editor-in-Chief of the literary magazine called PAPIRUS.

**Michael Speier** is a poet, literary scholar, and translator, living in Berlin. Having taught at the Freie Universität Berlin, the University at Leipzig, and several U.S. universities (Dartmouth College and Georgetown University among them). He is also Adjunct Professor at the German Department of the University of Cincinnati. In addition to having published a number of anthologies and translated modern English, French, and Italian poetry, he is the founding editor of the Paul-Celan-Jahrbuch and the literary magazine Park. He has published eleven volumes of poetry. His work has appeared in over 50 anthologies and has been translated into fourteen languages. In 2007 he received the Schiller Award (Weimar). He was awarded the Literaturpreis der A+A

Kulturstiftung (Köln) in 2011, and the Danube Award of the poetry festival Smederewo 2020. Member of PEN and of the Académie Mallarmé (Paris).
Translator Richard Dove was born in Bath/UK, and read Modern Languages at Oxford before teaching German and English at universities in England, Wales and southern Germany. Now living in Munich, he has published seven collections of poetry and several editions. He has also translated a number of German-speaking poets into English. Selected Poems 1946-2006, were shortlisted for the 2008 Oxford-Weidenfeld Translation Prize.

***Milica Jeftimijević Lilić*** graduated at the Faculty of Philosophy in Priština, and  won a master's degree in philological sciences at the University of  Belgrade. She was a professor at the University of  Priština, and editor on Belgrade TV. She has published collections of poems, stories and essays in 27 books. She is represented in many anthologies and has many literary awards of national importance   as international. Her  works translated into more than 28 languages of the world. She   used to be the vice-president of the Association of writers of Serbia Lives in Belgrade since 1999.


***Muberra Karamanoglu*** is a multidisciplinary artist based in Ankara, Turkey. Poet, writer, painter and sculptor. She also performs live performances called "Painting Poems"  where she combines poetry and painting. In 2015 her poetry book called    "Aramıza Şiir Kaçtı" was published. In 2019 participated in the 4th Intercontinental Young Poet İstanbul Festival  and International Literature Festival in Bistrita, Romania.

Her poems have been translated into English, Romanian and Spanish.


***Nurduran Duman*** is a poet, playwright, editor. Her poems have been translated into Finnish, Spanish, Azerbaijan Turkish, Bulgarian, Romanian, Slovak, French, German, Occitan, Italian. Modern Poetry in Translation (MPT) list of ten international female poets in translation in 2018. Member of Turkish PEN.
Translator Andrew Wessels has held fellowships from Poets & Writers and the Black Mountain Institute. Poems and translations by him can be found in VOLT, Kenyon Review, Witness, Tammy Journal, Faultline, and Colorado Review, among others.


***Padmaja Iyengar-Paddy*** is the Literary Coordinator (India), ISISAR, Kolkata, and the Editorial Counselor-India, International Writers' Journal, USA. Her maiden poetry collection 'P-En-Chants' has been recognized as a Unique Record of Excellence by the India Book of Records. Paddy has compiled and edited six international multilingual poetry anthologies of which 'Amaravati Poetic Prism' 2016 to 2019 have been recognized by the Limca Book of Records (published by Coca Cola India) as "Poetry Anthology in Most Languages". Paddy's poems, articles and short stories are regularly published in anthologies, magazines and e-zines.


***Raed Anis Al-Jish***i is an international awarded poet and a translator from Qateef-Saudi Arabia. He has an honorary fellowship in writing from Iowa University, USA, is a member of advisory committee of exquisite teacher training plan of national Changua University of Education-Taiwan and an editor in modern dialogs-Macedonia.

**Raquel Martínez-Gómez** has written six novels and five collections of poems. She has been awarded, among others, with the European Union Prize for Literature 2010 or the Antonio García Cubas´ Historical Novel Award (México, 2018). She has a PhD in International Relations and an MA in Modern and Contemporary Literature, Culture and Thought. Ana García-Casillas Martínez-Gómez is a young emerging Spanish writer based in Germany. She currently is doing a European Voluntary Service in a circus.

**Šimo Ešić** was born in 1954 in Breze near Tuzla (Bosnia and Herzegovina. He completed his studies of language and literature in 1976. His books have been translated into German, Swedish, Macedonian, Slovenian, Bulgarian, English and Albanian. He has received number of awards and honors. He was also nominated three times for the Astrid Lindgren Memorial Award (ALMA) the greatest book prize for children's literature in the World. He is a member of the Writers Society of Bosnia and Herzegovina, The German Writers' Association, The Society of Croatian Writers for Children and Youth. He lives as a freelance artist in Wuppertal (Germany) and Tuzla (Bosnia and Herzegovina).

**Simon Fletcher** lives in Shropshire, England, and is a widely published poet who's performed across Britain and in Pakistan, Norway and Germany. He's read his work on BBC Radio Shropshire and the BBC Asian Network. He runs poetry writing workshops in green spaces/places and MCs the monthly online Virtual Voices event. Author of three pamphlets and of four poetry collections, his most recent, Close to Home, published by Headland, 2015. Simon is also manager of Offa's Press, devoted to promoting and publishing poetry in the West Midlands of England.


**Simone Seym**, winner and inclusion in the Library of German-Language Poems Millennium Edition; recipient of the Lisa and Robert Kahn Poetry Prize 2020; member and poet of the Society for Contemporary American Literature in German. Simone went for three years to Japan, as a Professor with the German Academic Exchange Service, to research and follow the path of her most beloved poet Matsuo Bashō, the most famous poet of the Edo period in Japan, and the greatest master of haiku.


**Susanna Piontek** writes short stories, poetry, essays and book reviews. Her first book was translated into English and was published by Culicidae Press in 2011: "Have we possibly met before? And other stories." Publications in Germany, USA, Austria, Israel and Albania. Memberships: P.E.N. Centre of German-Speaking Writers Abroad, European Authors' Association "Die Kogge" and of SCALG (Society for Contemporary American Literature in German) Awards: SCALG Poetry Award (2015), SCALG Prose Award (2018).

**Utz Rachowski**, born 1954 in Saxony (Germany), was a former political prisoner in East Germany and was sentenced to 27 months jail because five of his own poems. He has published 14 books of stories, essays, and poetry. Most recently, he received the 2007 Reiner Kunze-Prize and the 2008 Hermann-Hesse-Stipendium. 2013; he was nominated for Pushcart Prize in the US 2014; Nikolaus-Lenau-Prize 2017; Geertje Potash-Suhr Prize for Prose and the Lisa & Robert Kahn Prize for Poetry, both from the Society for Contemporary American Literature in German.
Translator Louise E. Stoehr, born 1956 in Los Angeles, California, is Professor of German at Stephen F. Austin State University in Nacogdoches, Texas. She has published numerous literary translations.

**Uwe Friesel**, born 1939 in Germany, having staid for decades in Italy and Sweden, now lives as a freelance writer in Buxtehude, Germany. In the seventies founder of the AutorenEdition (AE) at C. Bertelsmann publishing house. He has published novels, short stories, poems, as well as youth- and children books and radio drama. He was awarded a number of literary awards, amongst them the prestigious Rome Prize Villa Massimo. After the Fall of the Berlin Wall, being president of the re-united German Writers' Union till 1994, he helped to organize the two international writers' cruises in the Baltic and Aegean Sea in 1992 and 1994, which resulted in the founding of the still active UNESCO writers' and translators' centers in Visby and Rhodes.

***Valentin Iacob*** (b. 1955) is a Romanian writer, poet and journalist, member of the Romanian Writers' Union. He has published several books of poetry. His poetry has been translated into English, Turkish, Hungarian and German.
The Translator George Volceanov (born in 1956) is a distinguished literary translator, lexicographer and professor of English literature in Bucharest. He has translated more than sixty books from English and Hungarian.


***Varsha Das*** writes fiction, non-fiction, poetry, radio plays and also for children in Gujarati, Hindi and English; and translates from Bengali, English, Gujarati, Hindi, Marathi and Odia. Her poems are included in several anthologies in India and abroad. She is a recipient of several literary awards notably the Kendra Sahitya Akademi Award, Lifetime Achievement Award from Gujarat Sahitya Parishad and literary award from the Soka University, Tokyo, Japan.  She is the former Director of National Book Trust, India and after her retirement served as the Director of National Gandhi Museum, New Delhi.


***William S. Peters, Sr.***, aka 'Just Bill', is an award-winning global activist for humanity. His poetry and prowess have been acknowledged and translated across the world. He is the founder and chair of Inner Child Enterprises, Inner Child Press International and the World Healing, World Peace Foundation. He utilizes these vehicles along with his poetry and other writings to champion the cause of consciousness, peace, love, acceptance and compassion. His personal perspective is that 'life is a garden', and we must plant seeds of good intent, light and love that we all may harvest a sweet bountiful fruit.

***Yin Xiaoyuan*** is founder of Encyclopedic Poetry School (est. 2007). She graduated from Beijing International Studies University, majoring in Japanese Literature. She is a member of Writers' Association of China, Translators' Association of China and Poetry Institute of China. She has published eleven books including five poetry anthologies.


***Yiorgos Chouliaras*** is a Greek poet, essayist, prose writer, and translator, honored by the Academy of Athens for his innovative writing and his work in its entirety. His poetry in translation has been published in leading U.S. periodicals and anthologies, and in Bulgaria, Croatia, France, Germany, India, Italy, Japan, Lithuania, Romania, Sweden, and Turkey among other countries. He has been elected President of the Hellenic Authors' Society, the principal association of literary writers in Greece.
Translator David Mason is an award-winning American poet, librettist, editor, critic, and university professor. A former Colorado poet laureate, he now lives in Tasmania with his wife, the poet Cally Conan-Davies (a.k.a. Chrissy Mason).


***Yuray Tolentino Hevia***. Poet, screenwriter, curator, art critic and producer. Graduate in Sociocultural Studies. He has obtained different awards and mentions: Finalist of the I Canibaal Hyperbreve Literature Contest, Spain, 2016; and International Award "Tulliola - Renato Filippelli", 2020, Italy. His work has been published in magazines, newspapers and poetry and narrative anthologies in Cuba, Spain,

Argentina, Chile, the United States, Italy and Mexico. Ambassador of Latin American Poetic Art in Cuba.

***Yuyutsu Sharma***. Sharma is a world renowned Himalayan poet and translator. He has published ten poetry collections. Three books of his poetry, have appeared in French,  Spanish and Slovenian respectively. He has held workshops in creative writing and translation at Queen's University, Belfast, University of Ottawa and South Asian Institute, Heidelberg University, Germany, University of California, Davis, Sacramento State University, California, Beijing Open University, New York University, New York and Columbia University, New York. In 2020, his work was showcased at Royal Kew Gardens in an Exhibit, "Travel the World at Kew."


***Zorin Diaconescu,*** graduate of the English Language Department of the Faculty of Letters – Babes-Bolyai University, Cluj, Romania. Building a bridge between Romanian and English – a job for a lifetime. Occasionally he writes poetry. He also published a documentary book about the year 1989, writes in and translates into from: Romanian, German and English.